Basic Stuff Series II

volume eight

The Basic Stuff in Action for Grades 4–8

Leslie T. Lambert
University of Wyoming

R. Thomas Trimble
University of Georgia

Contributing Authors:

Norma J. Carr
State University of New York at Cortland

Marian E. Kneer
University of Illinois at Chicago

Judith H. Placek
Boston University

a project of the
National Association for Sport and Physical Education
an association of the
**American Alliance for Health, Physical Education,
Recreation, and Dance**

BASIC STUFF SERIES

A collection of books presenting concepts, principles, and developmental ideas extracted from the body of knowledge for physical education and sport. Each book is intended for use by undergraduate majors and instructors in physical education.

BASIC STUFF SERIES

Series One: Information Books

Exercise Physiology (V1)
Kinesiology (V2)
Motor Learning (V3)
Psycho-Social Aspects of Physical Education (V4)
Humanities in Physical Education (V5)
Motor Development (V6)

Series Two: Learning Experience Books

The Basic Stuff in Action for Grades K–3 (V7)
The Basic Stuff in Action for Grades 4–8 (V8)
The Basic Stuff in Action for Grades 9–12 (V9)

Series II Editorial Committee

Norma J. Carr, Editor
SUNY: Cortland College
Cortland, New York

Elizabeth S. Bressan
University of Oregon
Eugene, Oregon

Marian E. Kneer
University of Illinois at Chicago
Chicago, Illinois

Barbara Lockhart, Consultant
University of Iowa
Iowa City, Iowa

R. Thomas Trimble
University of Georgia
Athens, Georgia

Preface

The *Basic Stuff* Series, a project of the National Association for Sport and Physical Education, was designed to encourage and support the idea that disciplinary knowledge about how and why the body moves is a worthwhile and appropriate aspect of the physical education curriculum. The *Basic Stuff* Series I and II were founded on the basis of the following assumptions:

1. a cognitive understanding about how and why people move is part of being "physically educated;"
2. active learning through physical participation in carefully designed learning experiences is paramount to a quality physical education program; and
3. there is no one best way to select and structure content for the physical education curriculum. The needs and interests of children in Kindergarten through Grade 12 differ, and the manner in which physical educators include cognitive understandings within the curriculum must reflect and be sensitive to those differences.

It is clear that students need to know the rules, terms, and strategies of games, sports, dance, gymnastics, and exercise activities if they are to perform in a competent manner. However, in order to be physically *educated,* a deeper understanding of movement participation is necessary. Students must grasp the reasons why certain things happen during participation. They must think about whether those things deal with what is happening to their bodies, their capacity to deal with force, and/or their interpersonal relationships with their peers.

Researchers are discovering new concepts in the subdisciplines of exercise physiology, motor learning, motor development, and kinesiology, as well as gaining new insights into the psycho-social aspects and the humanities perspective on physical activity. A highly specialized and sophisticated body of knowledge is now available. Physical educators are faced with the enormous task of analyzing these concepts in order to select those which are appropriate for inclusion in a school physical education program. The *Basic Stuff* Series I books attempt to identify those concepts from the subdisciplines which may become content for a physical education program. The Series II books (of which this volume is a part) select some of those concepts appropriate for different grade levels and provide learning experiences for classroom use by the physical educator.

The format of the books in Series II is intended to be practical, readable, and enjoyable. After an introduction with suggestions for incorporating cognitive concept learning into the physical education curriculum, three chapters, specific to each grade level, are provided for K–3, 4–8, and 9–12. Three goals have been selected: personal fitness is addressed in Chapter 3; skillful moving in Chapter 4; and joy, pleasure, and satisfaction is covered in Chapter 5. After a summary of the importance of including understandings for each goal, appropriate concepts from Series I are selected and active learning experiences are offered as content suggestions.

The development of the *Basic Stuff* Series was a unique, cooperative effort by teams of authors, instructional developers, and age group specialists from the public schools. Experts from the subdisciplines selected the content and were assisted in the development of instructional materials. Public school teachers certified relevance of the content to students, field tested various instructional activities, and encouraged the authors to write for general understanding.

This series is a collection of exciting new ideas for implementing concepts from the subdisciplines through active learning experiences. Central to the authors' intentions for *Basic Stuff*, however, is that the project be an ongoing, evolving one, with the teacher participating in its development. The learning experiences included can and should be adjusted and modified to tailor curriculum to the unique needs of specific students and programs. Considerations must be made about local facilities, available equipment, and the past experience of the students for whom the activity is being designed. Teachers are also encouraged to examine the information in the Series I books to find other concepts appropriate for their programs. By developing new learning experiences for these concepts and sharing them with other physical educators, the *Basic Stuff* project can continue to grow and meet the changing needs of the physical education profession.

Table of Contents

chapter one
Overview

The books in Series II of the *Basic Stuff* are organized according to the traditionally accepted grade levels of K–3, 4–8, and 9–12 and provide teaching-learning experiences appropriate for each of those levels. The concepts presented in the six books in Series I have been reviewed and assigned to a particular grade level according to the Editorial Board's opinion of "best fit." Attempts have been made to include some of the same concepts across the grade levels to provide a developmental scope. However, due to the vast number of relevant concepts identified in Series I books, not all concepts are included in Series II. These books provide concrete teaching-learning experiences for the included concepts and, in addition, should be viewed and utilized as models for designing teaching-learning experiences for other concepts presented in Series I.

This chapter provides an overview of the book and a general rationale for the approach. The curricular organization is centered on specific goals in addition to grade levels. It was the authors' assumption that most physical educators agree that personal fitness, skillful moving, and attention to the joy, pleasure, and satisfaction derived from physical activity are primary goals of a physical education program. Concepts suitable for these goals were clustered in three separate chapters. Teaching-learning experiences deemed appropriate for the specified grade levels were then designed.

Chapter 2 assists teachers with working *Basic Stuff* into their programs and offers suggestions about how it best may be incorporated. Teachers are provided with curriculum organizing centers followed by ways of designing teaching-learning experiences which may be integrated, segregated, or separated in each lesson. A discussion of action versus non-action experiences and suggested criteria for quality learning experiences are included. The teaching-learning experiences in Chapters 3 (personal fitness), 4 (skillful moving), and 5 (joy, pleasure, and satisfaction) may now be considered from the standpoint of action and non-action experiences and be measured against these criteria.

Personal Fitness

The most recent study conducted for the President's Council on Physical Fitness and Sports (1985), in conjunction with many previous studies, demonstrates that American youth continue to be unfit. Nearly half of our children aged 6–12 could not maintain their body weight in a chin over the bar position for more than ten seconds. Twenty-five per cent of the boys and 55% of the girls could not complete even one pull-up. Only 60% of the boys and 30% of the girls could complete more than one pull-up. Thirty per cent of the boys and 50% of the girls could not complete a mile run in fewer than 10 minutes. These statistics are not new, but merely reaffirm the condition of our youth as it was in

1965 and 1975. Our current physical education programs appear not to be challenging our students to increase strength, flexibility, and endurance. These findings underscore a serious curricular deficiency.

The President's Council Study has been released at a time when interest in fitness and adult participation in physical activity appears to be great. Americans seem to be concerned about health and fitness. Adults are changing their eating, drinking, and smoking habits and are participating in aerobic programs of all types. Yet our children are not following these examples. Parents assume that school physical education programs are providing their children with sound health habits and acceptable fitness levels, but the research demonstrates that this is not the case.

Concepts and the accompanying teaching-learning experiences presented in Chapter 3 of this book address the fitness goal. Personal fitness has a historical and philosophical tradition in physical education programs. This book will help physical educators encourage children and assist them in achieving an acceptable, if not exemplary, level of fitness, along with an understanding of the importance of physical activity in life.

Skillful Moving

The development of skill has long been established as a goal of physical education. The importance of efficient and effective movement in work and play, and in structured and unstructured movement patterns, is a primary focus. It is the belief of the *Basic Stuff* authors that a cognitive understanding of movement is an essential element in learning to move well. Knowing how and why movement occurs, and whether it is efficient and effective in solving problems, enhances understanding. The integration of the cognitive and psychomotor domains is the focus of Chapter 4. Teaching-learning experiences are presented which will aid students in skillful moving.

Joy, Pleasure, and Satisfaction

The third primary goal of physical education relates to that intangible, subtle, sometimes irrational, and frequently beautiful affective involvement that occurs when people move. An active lifestyle is sought by those whose past movement experiences were positive, or at least meaningful. The joy, pleasure, and satisfaction which accompany physical activity can have an exhilarating, positive effect on one's sense of self. Assisting children in their quest for aesthetically pleasing experiences when moving is discussed in Chapter 5, and teaching-learning experiences that address this goal are provided.

Using Series II

Each of the chapters dealing with the three goals begins with an introduction followed by a series of suggested teaching-learning experiences for concepts selected from the Series I books. Curriculum materials are provided in the form of worksheets, lab experiences, and out-of-class assignments. Full sized masters are included for making transparencies and duplicates. Finally, ideas for evaluating performance and under-standing are outlined. Teachers are encouraged to duplicate any or all materials provided.

The original Series I (1981) has been revised and contains some updates and changes. Verbatim concepts are selected from Series I and are cross referenced to this text. The concept is stated as it appears in Series I and is followed, for example, by (V5, P23). This indicates that a more detailed explanation of the concept is found in Book 5 on page 23 in Series I (1987). Series I (1981) users may contact AAHPERD for a cross reference sheet to the earlier edition.

Although it is possible to use the learning experiences in this book without referring to Series I, teachers are encouraged to use the two series together in order to provide the best learning conditions for students and the fullest understanding of the concepts. In some instances, related concepts are identified and reference made to the appropriate book in Series I which discusses these related concepts in more detail. Included at the end of each chapter is a blank copy of the outline used by the authors to present concepts and to design teaching-learning experiences. Teachers are urged to make copies of this outline and to develop further learning experiences on the same or related concepts or from an entirely new concept chosen from the books in Series I.

The *Basic Stuff* authors have not attempted to provide lesson and unit plans for all concepts, nor are all possible learning experiences presented for teaching a single concept. Teachers must, of necessity, adapt the lessons provided to individual situations in terms of class size, facilities, equipment, type of student, and the needs and interests of those students. The authors hope that many new ideas will be developed by the readers of these books. Users of Series II are encouraged to share their lessons and learning experiences by submitting them on the provided outline. Outlines received will be compiled and published by AAHPERD with proper credit given to the people who submitted the ideas.

Finally, this series has been carefully written by teachers for use by teachers. Because it is important to know people's reactions to the books, an evaluation form is included at the end of each book. Users are encouraged to submit comments on the series via this form. Future revisions will incorporate these user suggestions.

chapter two

Introduction of *Basic Stuff* as Part of Physical Education

Through the years, many physical educators have overlooked the importance of including concepts taken from our subdisciplines in the classroom. Some teachers may have felt that the shortage of time assigned for physical education has not permitted attention to this aspect of our curriculum. Others have felt that the changes to their programs would be overwhelming and complex. A conscious effort is being made in this chapter to assist those instructors and prospective instructors who agree that we can—and must—include our cognitive subdisciplinary concepts throughout the curriculum. When introducing *Basic Stuff* into an existing program, teachers must consider four key factors. First, the curriculum organizing centers must be identified. Second, teachers must work out the best lesson plan strategy for their individual situation. Third, they must determine the appropriate amounts of action and non-action experiences to include. And finally, the specific criteria to be followed when planning the learning experiences must be established. Following is a discussion of each of these factors, outlined to help teachers plan for the introduction of *Basic Stuff* concepts into their programs.

Curriculum Organization

The first step is to decide how the curriculum is to be organized. Generally, curricula tend to be activity centered, movement centered, motive centered, centered on subdiscipline areas, or eclectic.

The movement forms or activity as the organizing center is the most popular and traditional way of organizing content, at least for grades 4–12. Grades K–3 tend to use the movement analysis/movement concept organizing centers more frequently than do the upper grades. However, all of the organizing centers presented in Figure 1 are usable and all of the concepts from *Basic Stuff* can be incorporated in any type of curricular organization. In all cases, it is recommended that regardless of the organizing center, appropriate active experiences should be the primary focus of the lesson.

Approach for Planning Lessons

Although teachers may organize their curriculum in different ways and for different purposes, a conceptual grasp about what, how, and why people move is desirable and is a legitimate part of the goals of physical education. Thus, the next step to consider is the desired approach to including these concepts in lessons. Concepts can be *integrated* or *segregated* within a lesson or *separated* as a distinct unit (see Figure 2).

Integrating or segregating concepts is a lesson planning strategy in which the concepts are used within a planned unit of instruction. Integrating and segregating allow for more continuity of the lesson's focus by relating the concept to be learned to the skills and/or games being taught. Separating concepts is a lesson planning strategy that is utilized when the concepts to be learned are to be part of a specially designed, separate unit or mini-unit.

Figure 3 illustrates how teachers could use a games unit to integrate concepts taken from the Series I books. In the integrated plan, concept objectives from one or more of the subdisciplines are planned to be taught in the unit. In this illustration, the concepts are taken from *Kinesiology*. The lesson plan example presents the major components of the two lessons, without going into detail. Note how the kinesiology concept is to be taught. Opportunity is provided for individual exploratory movement, and problem solving questions are asked. Game C is selected to provide follow-up use of stability concepts and to give the students practice in using the concept "lowering the center of gravity" to gain stability. This is just one example of integrating concepts into a lesson. Since the unit content has the activity/movement form of games as an organizing center, the major part of the lessons are focused on that goal and not the stability concept.

Figure 4 illustrates the same organizing center approach, activity/movement form, but segregates the teaching-learning of Series I concepts into two or three lessons. The

1. ACTIVITY CENTERED		
Basketball	Archery	Games
Volleyball	Golf	Dance
Swimming	Tennis	Apparatus
2. MOVEMENT ANALYSIS / MOVEMENT CENTERED		
Force	Dynamics	Dodging
Balance	Creativity	Striking
Propelling	Life Survival	Hanging
3. MOTIVE / PURPOSE CENTERED		
Appearance	Aesthetics	
Health	Coping	
Achievement	Psycho-Social	
4. DISCIPLINE CENTERED		
Exercise Physiology	Motor Learning	
Body Mechanics	Motor Development	
Kinesiology	Sports Psychology	
Humanities	Sociology of Sport	
5. ECLECTIC		
Basketball	Humanities	
Dynamics	Golf	
Health	Apparatus	

Figure 1. Organizing centers for curriculum.

INTEGRATED:	One or more selected "Basic Stuff" concepts taught within a lesson.
SEGREGATED:	One or more complete "Basic Stuff" lessons which may or may not be related to current unit of study. Lesson may be taught with or without activity in a gymnasium or classroom.
SEPARATED:	"Basic Stuff" unit taught in whole.

Figure 2. Lesson plan strategies for teaching *Basic Stuff*.

LESSON #1	LESSON #2
Warm-up	Warm-up
Game A	Review Games A or B
Social Concept	Kinesiology Concept
Game B	Game C

LESSON PLAN #2 (The first lesson was taught previously)

TOPIC	ORGANIZATION and PROCEDURES	DISCUSSION	TIME
Warm-ups	Mike leads Scattered		3
Review Game A Game B	To be determined To be determined	To be determined To be determined	10
Kinesiology Concept Stability depends upon the height of the center of gravity (V2, P44)	Class explores various ways Partners apply force to test the position	Ask "How will this ability help you?"	5
Teach Game C	To be determined	Is stability important in this game? Why? How?	15
Cool Down	Usual Routine		5

Figure 3. Sequence plan for *integrated* teaching of *Basic Stuff*.

same games are taught as in Figure 3, but games and concepts are provided in separate lessons. Games are the focus of Lesson 1, while Lesson 2 focuses on the concepts. A subsequent lesson could be used as appropriate reinforcing experiences for the concepts.

A separated plan occurs only if the teacher wishes to focus the learning on knowledge rather than activity. Instead of an activity focus being integrated or segregated from knowledge, the entire unit and each lesson within the unit or mini-unit is focused on concepts. Activities, if any, are selected to reinforce knowledge but are not the major outcomes. It may be that the *Basic Stuff* project will inspire more curriculum planners to use subdiscipline concepts as the organizing center. Figure 5 presents an example of a

LESSON #1	LESSON #2
Warm-up	Warm-up
Game A	Humanities Concept and Activity
Game B	Kinesiology Concept and Activity
Game C	Exercise Physiology Concept and Activity

LESSON PLAN #2 (The first lesson was taught previously)

TOPIC	ORGANIZATION and PROCEDURES	DISCUSSION	TIME
Warm-ups	Susie leads Scattered		3
Humanities Concept What feels good differs among participants (V5, P1)	Explore what body can do: Walk, Run, Hop, etc. Make combinations	What does it feel like? How do you feel?	5
Kinesiology Concept Stability depends upon the height of the center of gravity (V2, P44)	Class explores various ways Partners apply force to test the position	Ask "How will this ability help you?"	10
Physiology Concept To be determined			10
Cool Down	Usual Routine		5

Figure 4. Sequence plan for *segregated* teaching of *Basic Stuff.*

concept unit and one lesson from that unit. The unit is planned around force generation concepts and the activities selected are the means to understanding the concept and its application to a variety of physical education activities. Selection of activities to teach these concepts is left to the planner's discretion. A variety of activities, or a single activity which has great potential to unite knowledge and activity, could be utilized.

The choice of integrating, segregating, or separating concepts within the lesson or unit plans rests with the teacher or curriculum designer. However, as teachers continue to implement the *Basic Stuff,* one integrating approach appears to have gained momentum. In an activity centered curriculum, such as softball (see Figure 6), many teachers use the following approach. First, in a softball unit, the teacher would list the skills to be taught, such as throwing, hitting, and bunting. After each skill, the teacher would list some concepts identified from Series I. For example, throwing may be the best activity to teach the motor learning concept about the speed versus accuracy trade off. Still relating to throwing, it also would be viable to teach the kinesiological concept of using a maximum number of body segments to increase force; or the exercise physiology concept regarding the role of strength in improving performance. Many additional concepts presented and discussed in Series I could be taught when teaching fielding, catching, or pitching. Teachers are encouraged to go through the curriculum and Series I books to identify at least one concept which may be taught appropriately in conjunction with each activity.

Cognitive concepts from the subdisciplines can—and must—be included in the physical education curriculum.

UNIT PLAN ON KINESIOLOGY

Objectives:
1. To identify and understand concepts relating to force.
2. To be able to apply force concepts to movement.

Monday	Tuesday	Wednesday	Thursday	Friday
Value of force How force is used Selected activities using force	Force Production Throwing, pushing, lifting, kicking	Understanding force Trying out amounts and variation on a variety of physical activity	Role of body in force production Apply to selected body movements	External production of force Exploring wind, gravity, and speed effects on body and objects
Understanding External force Exploring effects on selected activities and movements	Application of force Experiencing the principles of force on hitting, throwing, pushing, kicking	Absorbtion of force Catching, stopping type activities	Force and Direction Experiencing differences in direction with force application	Application of direction of force on objects Rebounding, landing type activities
Force and spin Trying to spin stationary and moving objects	Force and body rotation Rotation activities	Force and speed Running, jumping, and throwing activities	Skill tests on force principles to throwing, hitting, catching, and kicking	Written test on force

LESSON PLAN from the above KINESIOLOGY UNIT (Lesson on Wednesday, Week 2)

Objectives:
1. To understand how to absorb force.
2. To apply force absorbtion principles to catching and stopping type activities.

TOPIC	ORGANIZATION & PROCEDURES	DISCUSSION	TIME
Warmups	Go to assigned places. Rotate when finished	None	5 Min.
Review external factors on force	Complete task sheet on exploring effects on movements.	Why does it work? What can you do?	10 Min.
Body position and absorbtion of force	Throw against wall, net, to other . . . increase distance. Make hands act like a net to absorb force. Throw balloons filled with water	What happens? Stress increasing size of receiving area and bringing hands in	15 Min.
Cool down	Usual routine	None	5 Min.

Figure 5. Unit and lesson plan for *separated* teaching of *Basic Stuff*.

UNIT: SOFTBALL

SKILLS TO LEARN	VOLUME	CONCEPT
Throwing	*Motor Learning* *Kinesiology* *Exercise Physiology*	Practice for speed, for accuracy, or for both as the skill requires (V3, P30) Use maximum number of body segments to increase force (V2, P55) Adequate strength and muscle endurance are necessary in many activities (V1, P2)
Hitting	*Kinesiology*	The amount of available force for striking is governed by the amount of muscular force, timing of body movements, length of striking implement, and firmness of grip (V2, P59)
Bunting Fielding Catching Pitching	*Kinesiology*	Spin results when force is applied off center of the object (V2, P33)
Strategy Rules Tournament	*Humanities*	Competition depends on cooperation (V5, P24)

Figure 6. Including *Basic Stuff* in activity centered units.

Figure 7 illustrates additional activity units in which teachers have included three or four concepts from *Basic Stuff* Series I books. The focus of the unit is on the specific activity, yet the inclusion of the concepts enriches the unit and improves students' understandings.

A systematic approach for the inclusion of concepts can be accomplished by good record keeping. A record of concepts planned for implementation in a specific activity unit will aid in avoiding duplication of the concepts and will insure a variety from the six books in Series I. Figure 8 provides a sample planning sheet for introducing *Basic Stuff* into your program. Across the top of the planning sheet are the book titles and numbers. In this illustration, teachers decide to include four humanities concepts and six motor learning concepts.

Learning Experiences

There are two major types of learning experiences for teaching concepts: *action* and *non-action*. The action types include problem solving, experiencing, creating, and exploring. Non-action types include comparing, planning, observing, charting, and reading. It is recommended that action type learning experiences be emphasized, although there is a place for non-action types as well. Teachers teaching the concept that "a projectile moves under the influence of the imparted force" might choose the following learning experiences:

Action:	"Roll the ball."	(Explore)
Non-Action:	"See the effects of different speeds."	(Observe)
Action:	"Roll hula hoops with backspin so that they will return."	(Experience)
Non-Action:	"Read about how to apply spin."	(Read)

Another concept, for example, is "Looking good is dynamic, not static." Two suggested learning experiences could be:

Non-Action:	"Discuss photos and traits and then observe each other during class activity for those characteristics and traits.	(Observe)
	Identify model performances that demonstrate a dynamic,	(Plan)
	athletic look."	(Compare)
Action:	"Work in small groups. Plan and act out a performance	
	which will pantomime the beauty of an activity."	(Experience)

UNIT: Folk Dance

VOLUME	CONCEPTS
Kinesiology	Smaller strides increase stability on slippery surfaces (V2, P68)
Psycho-Social Aspects	Aesthetic movement experiences help an individual feel good (V4, P10)
Motor Learning	Mental practice can improve performance (V3, P35)

UNIT: Volleyball

VOLUME	CONCEPTS
Psycho-Social Aspects	Fear of failure affects performance in physical activity (V4, P20)
Motor Development	Development of body awareness, balance, spatial awareness, and tactile location aids performance (V6, P29)
Kinesiology	Force is needed to produce or change motion (V2, P1)
Humanities	Specific activities emphasize different characteristics of beauty (V5, P9)

UNIT: Tennis

VOLUME	CONCEPTS
Kinesiology	Force will be reduced if firm contact is not maintained at the moment of contact or release (V2, P49)
Kinesiology	A follow through facilitates projection at maximum velocity (V2, P49)
Psycho-Social Aspects	Self-talk can aid in doing better (V4, P34)

Figure 7. Additional activity centered units including *Basic Stuff* concepts.

V1 EXERCISE PHYSIOLOGY	V2 KINESIOLOGY	V3 MOTOR LEARNING	V4 PSYCHO- SOCIAL ASPECTS	V5 HUMANITIES	V6 MOTOR DEVEL- OPMENT
Need for strength (P2)	Need for force (P1)	Practice conditions (P51)	Freedom (P10)	Beauty (P7)	Growth (P17)
Measuring strength (P12)	Muscles and force (P2)	Performance factors (P55)	Subjectivity (P24)	Competition (P23)	Perception (P26)
Anaerobic training (P16)	Flexing & extending (P4)	Timing (P70)	Affiliation (P40)	Cooperation (P24)	Body Differences (P31)
Aerobic endurance (P19)	Muscles and force (P13)	Feedback (P77)	Aggression (P46)	Form (P35)	Form and performance (P42)
Flexibility (P33)	Gravity (P24)	Cue Discrimination (P95)	Arousal (P57)		Goals (P54)
Fitness and fatigue (P74)	Controlling Rebound (P29)	Chunking (P100)	Self-Control (P58)		Improvement (P56)
Value of activity (P79)	Spin (P32)				
	Body Rotation (P39)				
	Stability (P42)				
	Velocity (P48)				

Figure 8. Planning worksheet for including *Basic Stuff* concepts in physical education.

Criteria and Strategies for Designing Learning Experiences

Five criteria to insure quality learning experiences when introducing *Basic Stuff* into your program are:

1. Provide action
2. Provide for ability differences
3. Provide for high incentives: fun and challenging for all
4. Provide for success for all students
5. Results in knowledge and understanding

Although learning experiences are either action or non-action, each lesson should provide some action type activities. How much action will depend on personal preference, type of concept, teacher's and students' objectives, and a myriad of other considerations. The learning experience will be more successful if it provides a range of tasks which will allow for ability differences. Certainly, if the task for applying force calls for strength that is far above or far below the level of the student, the experience will lack meaning for those who are at the extremes. Likewise, the task should offer high incentive by being fun and challenging for all students. This calls for sensitivity to the students' interests and needs, while keeping the goal of the task within a range that is achievable for all students. This criteria may require variable goals or tasks specified for certain ability levels. And finally, the learning experience should result in learning the concept. Recall experiences and follow up applications should be planned to determine the effectiveness of the learning experience. Several examples of learning experiences can be seen in Figure 9.

In addition to the above criteria for creating or planning learning experiences, there are specific strategies to be used in teaching students:

1. Stress the focus of the lesson
2. Identify a concept related to the activity
3. Review the concept
4. Plan for transfer
5. Include the selected concept in evaluation mechanisms

Stressing the major focus of the lesson depends upon the curriculum model being used. If it is activity centered, such as throwing, stress throwing; if it is motive centered, such

---

VOLUME:	Humanities (V5)
CONCEPT:	Achievement may be based on the comparison with others or self and accomplishment (V5, P15)
ACTIVITY:	Dance

LEARNING EXPERIENCE:

1. Teach a dance pattern without accompaniment and have students perform in small groups or with a partner.

2. Have students select accompaniment and rearrange the pattern for their group. Demonstrate the dance to the rest of the class.

3. Discuss. How do you feel about your dance? About others' dances? Does it matter?

VOLUME:	Motor Learning (V3)
CONCEPT:	Skills are classified in various ways (V3, P16)
ACTIVITY:	Basketball

LEARNING EXPERIENCE:

1. Define and discuss open and closed skill differences.

2. Ask students to give examples of sports and to classify them as open or closed.

3. Compare different basketball skills such as a free throw, layup, jump shot, and set shot.

Figure 9. Sample learning experiences from *Basic Stuff Proceedings.* AAHPERD Pre-Convention Workshop, Anaheim, California, 1984, p. 24, 27.

as health, stress health. If the focus is concept centered, the major focus would be the specific concept. Students should know that they are being taught a movement concept and how that concept might transfer.

The important concepts should be stressed during active, physical performance. Strategies for teaching these concepts should be planned and the concepts, themselves, reviewed often with the students. Review is as important when teaching concepts as when teaching sport skills. If the concept has application two weeks or two months later in another unit, strategies for the transfer of the concept to the new activity must be consciously incorporated in that lesson. If written tests are given, include questions which cause the students to recognize, recall, or apply the concept.

Conceptual learning should be assessed just as skills, fitness levels, and sport knowledge are measured to assess the extent of learning. Measurement of concept learning also can be achieved through skill tests which focus on relevant knowledges. For example, the test may be to demonstrate where force must be applied to achieve different spins on objects.

Cognitive understandings can and should become a part of all physical education instructional plans. To assist in the effort of developing physically educated people, many additional examples of *action* and *non-action* conceptual learning experiences are provided in Chapters 3, 4, and 5 of this book.

photo by Greg Merhar

chapter three
Personal Fitness

Fitness education has a rather limited past. Historically, teachers have "exercised" students, caring little about personal meaning and more about the goal, albeit short-sighted, of becoming physically fit. Unfortunately, several by-products have resulted from this approach. Indeed, some students have achieved fitness under such command, but ended up with great distaste for the process. Additionally, this approach has created a large group of children who have not achieved, and do not understand, the basic principles of fitness.

For fitness education to work, several premises must be accepted. First, fitness can be planned for and gained through developmentally appropriate skill experiences. One approach does not preclude the other; programs must be comprehensive. To the degree that both skill and fitness are integrated, physical education programs will improve.

Second, students can learn how to be responsible for their own fitness development. The emphasis must be on encouraging and rewarding student involvement and facilitating their pursuit of self-management. Providing accurate information, creating exciting fitness environments, encouraging responsibility, and emphasizing a lifelong perspective all help contribute to the potential success of each student.

Third, for fitness to be gained and maintained, fitness experiences must be continually included in our programs. Unlike acquiring motor skill, fitness requires constant pursuit. There is no season for fitness. If students are to become physically fit and to understand the process of developing an active lifestyle, programs must provide a consistent message, directly and indirectly. Programs that offer one unit of fitness and do not incorporate fitness experiences consistently throughout the program are not only missing the point, but are giving an erroneous message to students. Fitness experiences must be integrated into every lesson and curricular content must be thoughtfully analyzed and modified in order to assure that fitness develops.

It is a myth that children are active enough on their own to gain proper physical conditioning. Depending on the criteria used to measure levels of fitness, well over half of this country's elementary school children can be considered unfit. Teachers *must* respond. They must place emphasis on cardiovascular development, and provide safe range of motion and strength activities while improving balance, coordination, and specific skills. Programs must fit the child, and not vice versa. If programs are progressive in demand, challenging, but not overwhelming, individually sensitive, organized for success, and provide a tangible plan for improvement, they will better encourage students toward seeking a lifetime of physical activity.

Topic: Health Related and Performance Related Fitness

Physical activity helps to turn on (V1, P90)

Adequate physical fitness is necessary in order to fully appreciate life. We all need an adequate fitness level to respond to emergencies. We also need to be physically fit to participate in leisure pursuits. Physical fitness may be classified as either health related or performance related. Components of health related fitness are:

1. cardiorespiratory endurance
2. muscular strength and endurance
3. flexibility
4. body composition

Performance related fitness includes components such as:

1. speed
2. agility
3. power
4. strength
5. endurance
6. balance

Health related fitness components are dynamic, important for good health, and can be improved considerably. Performance related fitness components are, for the most part, genetically imposed, important for athletic perform-ance, and may be improved slightly.

Both types of fitness are important and each separate component requires specific attention. Therefore, it is important to understand the differences between health related and performance related fitness and exactly what types of activities help enhance each component. As a result of this learning experience, the student will:

1. Be able to distinguish between health related and performance related fitness.
2. Better understand how to choose activities to enhance health related and performance related components.

Learning Experiences:

Physical Fitness

1. Review information in the discussion section.
2. Define each fitness component on the "Physical Fitness Components Log" sheets and give examples. Have students suggest examples.
3. A minimum of 15–20 minutes of continuous aerobic activity is necessary at least 3 times per week to enhance cardiorespiratory endurance and to maintain or improve body composition. To improve strength, a three day per week (every other day) routine seems best. Speed, agility, and balance need to be worked on regularly. Gaining and maintaining fitness takes time, effort, and an understanding of the components of physical fitness.
4. Each student should keep a physical fitness log. All physical activity can be characterized according to the components of fitness. Logs could be turned in each week or on a periodic basis.

Materials Needed:

"Physical Fitness Components Log"

Evaluation:

The teacher may evaluate this experience by comparing the activity performed with the fitness components the student checked.

PHYSICAL FITNESS COMPONENTS LOG

Name: _____ Class: _____

Instructor: _____ Period: _____

| DATE | TIME | HEART RATE | FITNESS COMPONENTS* | | | | | | | | ACTIVITY |
			CV	MS	ME	FL	SP	AG	BAL	POW	
6/10	10:00–10:20	150	✔								Jog
6/11	5:00– 5:15	120		✔		✔					Situps, Pushups & Flexibility Exercise

*CV = Cardiovascular Endurance   SP = Speed
MS = Muscular Strength   AG = Agility
ME = Muscular Endurance   BAL = Balance
FL = Flexibility   POW = Power

Topic: Fitness Development Through Games

Physical activity provides social benefits (V1, P85)

Often fitness activities (e.g. jogging, cycling, swimming) are thought of as solitary activities with little social interaction. Additionally, many teachers do not design instructional fitness experiences that are fun and include a social dimension. For fitness to be enjoyable and for students to be attracted to an active lifestyle, careful planning must be given to fitness experiences.

Fitness games provide both fun and social interaction. Many games and sports offer vigorous challenges for students and promote cooperation and competition. The activity, however, must be appropriate relative to motor skill and fitness ability. Further, the social benefit of working with others must be stressed.

As a result of this learning experience, the student will:

1. Be able to have fun while gaining fitness.
2. Understand that there are many ways to enhance aerobic improvement.

Learning Experiences:

Simple Aerobic Fitness Games

There are many games that enhance aerobic fitness. The main objective is to keep the students moving, practicing skills, and having fun. Other games can be modified in order to create aerobic challenges.

1. *Stomp!:* Partner or Small Group
   a. Tie three or four balloons on a long string. Attach the string to a belt loop or belt.
   b. Move around the area attempting to STOMP the balloons of others while protecting your own.

2. *Keep 'Em Moving:* Whole Class
   Using at least 40 tennis balls for a class of 20 students, scatter the balls around the gym. The object is to keep all the balls moving simultaneously by tapping the balls with the inside of the foot.

3. *Life Rafts:* Whole Class
   a. Scatter hula hoops (life rafts) around the activity area. Students jog around the rafts until "Overboard" is called. Object: Place one hand in the raft for safety.
   b. Gradually take away hoops until only one or two remain. Students may need to hold on to other players already on the raft.

   Monitor target heart rate to reinforce aerobic concerns.

Materials Needed:

- Stomp!: balloons, string
- Keep 'Em Moving: tennis balls
- Life Rafts: hula hoops
- pace clock

Evaluation:

When playing aerobic games it is important to explain *why* these activities enhance aerobic fitness. Students should periodically monitor their heart rates. Ideally, students should have the opportunity to remain actively involved in fitness games for at least 15–20 minutes.

Related Concepts:

- Participation in physical activity can be an important way of meeting affiliation needs (V4, P38)
- Affiliation is a very important human need (V4, P37)

Topic: Anaerobic and Aerobic Energy Sources

Anaerobic and Aerobic Production of ATP (V1, P28)

A muscle chemical, adenosine triphosphate (ATP), provides the energy for muscles to work. When ATP is produced via oxygen use, it is being produced aerobically. This aerobic production of ATP takes about four minutes to occur. In the meantime, three other sources of energy are providing ATP anaerobically (without oxygen): 1) creatine phosphate, 2) stores of raw ATP, and 3) muscle glycogen. Therefore, in order to produce and use energy aerobically, an individual must exercise for a period of time sufficient to allow the body's energy systems to respond.

Activities which utilize primarily anaerobic energy are short in length and strenuous in nature. Activities such as sprinting and gymnastic routines are good examples. Such activities usually range in time from 5 seconds to 2 minutes. Activities which allow the body to produce and use energy aerobically are long in duration and moderate in intensity. Jogging, cross country skiing, and fitness swimming are good examples.

As a result of this learning experience students should:

1. Be able to discern the difference between aerobic and anaerobic activity choices.
2. Be able to recognize the effort qualities of both aerobic and anaerobic activity experiences.

Learning Experiences:

Differentiating Between Aerobic and Anaerobic Energy Use

1. Discuss the concepts in the discussion section.
2. Students will monitor target heart rate (THR). During anaerobic activities heart rate may approach maximum levels (approximately 220 − age). Students should have prior knowledge of how to monitor heart rate and what their THR is.
3. Students should be asked to pay attention to how they feel relative to effort expended. How does heart rate respond? How is duration affected by intensity of exercise?
4. The "Task Sheet" explains all necessary information about the activity. Task sheets should be provided for each student. Students may work as individuals, partners, or in small groups. Each student should respond to each activity on the task sheet.

Materials Needed:

- "Task Sheets" and pencils
- pace clock
- mats for sit-ups
- basketballs
- four square "courts" and balls
- jump ropes

Evaluation:

An end of class discussion would help further clarify differences in aerobic and anaerobic activities. Reviewing each student's task sheet after class will provide the teacher with individual evaluative information. Were heart rates consistent with activity intensity? Did students appropriately describe activities as mostly aerobic and anaerobic?

Related Concepts:

- Anaerobic training must be task-specific (V1, P16)
- Anaerobic performance can be measured to determine training effect (V1, P17)
- Anaerobic performances utilize three non-oxidative sources of ATP (V1, P18)

Task Sheet

Anaerobic and Aerobic Discovery Activity

Name _____

Instructions: Choose four different activities from those listed below. Write each activity on one of the lines provided below. Perform each activity in the specified range of time. As soon as you stop each activity, monitor and record your target heart rate. Rate each activity on the continuum from being mostly aerobic to being mostly anaerobic.

Activity Choices: 1. Walk briskly for 5–7 minutes
2. Do sit-ups for 2 minutes
3. Jog for 4–6 minutes
4. Perform fast lay-up drills for 3–4 minutes
5. Perform the vertical jump for height for 2–3 minutes
6. Play four square for 5–7 minutes
7. Practice the two hand over head pass against the wall or with a partner for 4–5 minutes
8. Jog and jump rope around the gym for 5–7 minutes

Record of Activities:

Activity Example: *Running Fast* the length of the gym four times
Heart rate: *190*
Mostly Aerobic_____/ Mostly Anaerobic_____

Activity 1: _____
HR: _____
Mostly Aerobic_____ Mostly Anaerobic_____

Activity 2: _____
HR: _____
Mostly Aerobic_____ Mostly Anaerobic_____

Activity 3: _____
HR: _____
Mostly Aerobic_____ Mostly Anaerobic_____

Activity 4: _____
HR: _____
Mostly Aerobic_____ Mostly Anaerobic_____

Topic: Aerobic Endurance

Aerobic endurance is needed for long periods of rhythmic low intensity muscle contractions (V1, P19)

Aerobic endurance can be improved in most healthy individuals. Though somewhat limited by genetic factors, one's aerobic capacity can improve significantly via proper activity. Activities can be designed to enhance aerobic endurance. Students should be taught the four basic elements of aerobic training: mode, intensity, duration, and frequency.

Developing a basic understanding of each of these four elements is important. The mode of exercise should involve large muscle groups simultaneously. The intensity (how hard to exercise) of the activity should be moderate (Target Heart Rate 150–170) and heart rate should be monitored. The duration (amount of time to exercise) of the activity should range from 15–45 minutes. The frequency (how often) should range from 3 to 5 days per week.

As much as is possible, the physical education program should provide aerobic exercise mode choices for students within lessons as well as across the entire curriculum. The elements of intensity, duration, and frequency should be adhered to regardless of the mode of activity.

As a result of these learning experiences, the students should:

1. Be able to pace themselves relative to the elements of intensity, duration, and mode of exercise.
2. Be able to monitor and determine Target Heart Rate.

Learning Experiences:

A: Monitoring and Determining Target Heart Rate

1. Make a chart for the wall that shows heart rate ranges for different ages and resting heart rates. This chart should be based upon the Karvonen heart rate reserve formula: Target Heart Rate = .60/.75 (Maximum Heart Rate* − Resting Heart Rate) + Resting Heart Rate. Have students take their resting heart rates at night before going to sleep for several nights. The average resting heart rate is 72 beats per minute. Taking their heart rate over a period of time and averaging it out will provide a reasonably accurate resting heart rate for each student. Teach students how to use the chart and monitor their pulse.

* Maximum Heart Rate = 220 − age

2. To monitor the pulse, place the 2nd and 3rd fingers on the thumb side of the wrist or on one side of the windpipe on the carotid artery. (If using the carotid artery, students should be taught not to apply pressure, but to merely find the pulse.) Exercise heart rate should be taken *immediately* after completing exercise. If the student waits more than a few seconds, the heart rate will not be accurate. Counting the pulse for a period of 6 seconds makes calculations simple. Count each beat for the 6-second period and put a zero at the end of that number in order to create a 60-second heart rate (17 beats in 6 seconds = 170 beats/minute). It will take a bit of practice, but students become proficient at this task in no time!

3. To practice this skill, have students perform different types of exercise for a few minutes—rope jumping, jogging, jumping jacks, and so on. Stop them all at the same time and provide a 6-second count for them. As they become proficient with this skill, they can become self-sufficient by watching a pace clock or the second hand on their watches.

4. Provide "Individual Heart Rate Logs" for students to record (a) periodic resting heart rates, (b) target heart rate during physical education class, and (c) target heart rates during after school and weekend activities.

B. Setting the Pace for Aerobic Endurance Activities

1. Discuss the concept with the students.
2. Explain what pacing means and relate to both intensity and duration principles.
3. Give students an idea of what the activity will "feel" like:
   a. Students should be able to carry on a conversation with a jogging partner.
   b. Upper body should be as relaxed as possible.
   c. Review proper foot to ground contact (heel-to-toe). This assumes a previous lesson on running form has been presented.
4. The teacher or designated student leader should establish a slow-to-moderate pace (10 to 12 minute mile pace) around the largest circumference of the teaching area. Students should follow in pairs in order to meet the 3a. criteria above. A follow-the-leader format may be followed (performing different locomotor activities and arm movements) and the pathway of the class may be altered at any time. Depending upon the size of the class, several groups may be formed. Once the pace has been established, the rear pair of participants jog briskly to the front of the line and reestablishes the pace. The objective is to move at an intensity suitable for aerobic conditioning for a specific period of time (5 minutes to start with). Students have a difficult time understanding "feeling" the effort expenditure needed to improve aerobic endurance. Students should check their heart rate immediately after stopping and it should be in the appropriate range. A brief discussion should follow this experience to reinforce the "feelings" as denoted in #3.

Note: A pace clock for the teaching area is very handy. Teach students to use it. It removes the stopwatch from the teachers' hands and frees them to participate and be more involved in teaching. Additionally, it helps create a self management atmosphere that encourages responsibility and self-testing.

C. Pacing—Estimated Time of Arrival

After experiencing a series of aerobic endurance activities and completing Learning Experience B, challenge the students with this task. Provide each student with a 3 × 5 index card with the following categories on it:

Name: _____ Group: _____

Estimated Time of Arrival: _____

Halfway Time: _____

Total Time: _____

Divide the class into small groups of about 4 or 5 students. A designated leader paces each group for given distance, let's say one-half mile. The group pace should not exceed a 10 minute per mile pace. (In order to establish this, the teacher may wish to provide the lead.) At the halfway point each group is given its time. Assuming all students reach the halfway point (one-half mile, in this instance) somewhere around 5 minutes and that they maintain their pace, their total time would be around 10 minutes. The students' objectives are:

- to be able to talk with jogging partners
- their estimated time of arrival (total) should be their halfway time multiplied by 2
- to maintain a consistent pace over the distance

The teacher may consider giving a prize to the group closest to their estimated time of arrival.

Materials Needed:

A.
- wall chart of target heart rates
- stopwatch
- jump ropes
- other equipment deemed necessary for exercise
- "Individual Heart Rate Logs"

B.
- stopwatch or pace clock
- wall chart of target heart rates

C.
- 3 × 5 index cards for estimated time of arrival
- pencils
- stopwatch or pace clock

Evaluation:

A.
The teacher may evaluate this activity in two ways. One is to randomly select several students and monitor their pulse along with them and compare. A second method would be to examine each student's "Individual Heart Rate Log" to see if resting heart rates and target heart rates are within common ranges.

B & C.
Pacing is a difficult concept for students to understand. The teacher should evaluate Learning Experiences B1 and B2 relative to students' ability to establish an appropriate jogging pace and their understanding of the process. Experience B2 can be further evaluated based upon individuals' estimated time of arrival information.

Related Concepts:

- Training must be progressive (V1, P23)
- Aerobic endurance improves maximal oxygen uptake (V1, P28)
- Fatigue is minimized through fitness (V1, P77)

AEROBIC ENDURANCE

Mode of Activity	Vigorous, rhythmic activity that simultaneously engages large groups of muscles (jogging, fitness swimming, cross country skiing, cycling, games/sports meeting these criteria, etc.)
Intensity	Target Heart Rate Target Heart Rate = .75 (Maximum Heart Rate − Resting Heart Rate) + Resting Heart Rate
Duration	15 to 45 minutes
Frequency	3 to 5 days per week

TARGET HEART RATE ZONE FOR
DIFFERENT AGES AND RESTING HEART RATES*

Resting Heart Rate	Age 6–10 years	Age 11–15 years
45–49	146–170	143–166
50–54	148–171	145–167
55–59	150–172	147–168
60–64	152–173	149–169
65–69	154–174	151–170
70–74	156–175	153–171
75–79	158–176	155–172
80–84	160–177	157–173
85–89	162–178	159–174

*Target zone is based upon age range and resting heart rate range. The 60 and 75 percent thresholds of the Karvonen heart rate reserve constitute the range.

Individual Heart Rate Log

Name: _____ Class: _____

Age: _____

Target Heart Rate Range: _____

Resting Heart Rate

September	_____	_____	_____	_____	=	_____
						Average
October	_____	_____	_____	_____	=	_____
						Average
November	_____	_____	_____	_____	=	_____
						Average
December	_____	_____	_____	_____	=	_____
						Average

Activity Record

Date	Type of Training	Duration	Heart Rate	Condition	Comments (Ex: felt good, easy today, too far, etc.)
6/1	Jog	30 min	160	Great!	Didn't stretch out enough—tight

Topic: Aerobic Endurance

Aerobic endurance training increases the stroke volume of the heart (V1, P32)

Aerobic endurance is enhanced by engaging in moderate intensity (150–170 beats per minute) activities that involve large groups of muscles simultaneously. Doing sit-ups is not a good choice to improve aerobic endurance. Even though heart rate may reach target levels or higher while doing sit-ups, large muscle groups are not working at the same time. Mainly abdominal muscles are engaged. Swimming the front crawl stroke continuously for 15 minutes or more is a good choice for improving aerobic endurance because leg, hip, back, abdominal, and upper body muscles are working together to move the body through the water. This type of activity creates a large volume demand on the cardiovascular system in addition to increasing the heart rate. In order to increase aerobic endurance, activities which not only elevate heart rate but also provide a large volume demand are needed.

As a result of this activity the student should:

1. Be able to distinguish between activities which create an increase in heart rate *only* and activities which increase heart rate *and* engage large groups of muscles to create a volume demand.
2. Be able to determine which activities are the best choices for enhancing aerobic endurance.

Learning Experiences:

Selecting Activities for Aerobic Endurance

1. Discuss the concepts from the discussion section.
2. Indicate that the activities planned should be analyzed as to their creation of aerobic demand, that is, heart rate *and* large muscle groups working together.
3. This experience will require monitoring target heart rate while doing various types of activities. Students should be able to determine which activities increase the workload on the cardiovascular system the most (and the least).
4. "Task Sheets" should be provided for each student and students should complete them independently. The task sheet provides an adequate explanation of this activity.

Materials Needed:

- "Task Sheets" and pencils
- jump ropes
- basketballs
- scooter boards
- traffic cones and other equipment to designate pathways for the obstacle courses

Evaluation:

Spending a bit of time talking about this activity at the end of class would provide general evaluative feedback. Checking each task sheet would offer the teacher further insight into each student's understanding of this concept.

Related Concepts:

- Aerobic endurance is needed for long periods of rhythmic low intensity muscle contractions (V1, P19)
- Aerobic endurance improves maximal oxygen uptake (V1, P28)

In order to increase aerobic endurance, activities which not only elevate heart rate but also provide a large volume demand are needed.

Task Sheet
Selecting Aerobic Endurance Activities

Name: _____

The best aerobic endurance activity choices should:
1. Increase your heart rate. In terms of intensity, a good target heart rate (THR) would be 150–170 beats.
2. Work large groups of muscles at the same time.

Perform each of the following activities for one minute. Take your 6-second THR and record it. Also, think about what parts of your body are working together. Is the workload on your heart *small, moderate,* or *large?*

Check (✔) the two activities that you feel are the *best* aerobic endurance choices.
Cross (X) the two activities that you feel are *not the best* aerobic endurance choices.
Can you suggest an activity we did not do that would be a *good* aerobic endurance choice?

1. Jump rope for one minute.

_____   _____
      6-second THR   Workload
                                 Small   Moderate   Large

2. Jog around the outside of the gym for one minute.

_____   _____
      6-second THR   Workload
                                 Small   Moderate   Large

3. Do sitting toe touches (Hamstring Stretch) for one minute.

_____   _____
      6-second THR   Workload
                                 Small   Moderate   Large

4. Dribble the basketball through the obstacle course for one minute.

_____   _____
      6-second THR   Workload
                                 Small   Moderate   Large

5. Do push-ups (or modified push-ups) for one minute.

_____   _____
      6-second THR   Workload
                                 Small   Moderate   Large

6. Sit on a scooter board and move yourself through the obstacle course for one minute.

_____   _____
      6-second THR   Workload
                                 Small   Moderate   Large

Topic: Interval Training

Aerobic endurance is tested by speed or distance in a given time frame (V1, P25)

Many activities require both aerobic and anaerobic fitness. If individuals only participate in continuous, moderate intensity level activities, anaerobic capacity does not improve significantly. Interval training, characterized by periods of high intensity work interspersed with periods of recovery, is a method of improving anaerobic fitness. Additionally, endurance capacity is enhanced.

Interval training workouts are designed based on the overload principle. The overload is created in one of four ways:

1. speeding up the pace of the work interval
2. decreasing the rest interval
3. increasing the distance of each work interval
4. increasing the number of repetitions

For beginners, setting up a program based on distance or repetitions is better.

Generally, when performing the work interval, heart rate should approach maximal levels. During the recovery interval, heart rate should decrease to between 120–140 beats per minute. Several repetitions should be done.

As a result of these learning experiences, the students will:
1. Be able to determine an appropriate interval training regime based on their one mile run time.
2. Understand the work/recovery ratio.

Learning Experiences:

A. Setting up an Interval Training Program Based on One Mile Run Time

1. Explain the concept of interval training.
2. Provide students with their one mile run times. Have them determine their 220 yard and 440 yard suggested pace based on their one mile run time.
3. Have students record their plans on 5 × 8 cards.

B. Relays as Interval Training

1. Relays are often used in physical education programs. They promote cooperation as well as competition. Students tend to enjoy the competition as long as the skill or fitness ability required by the relay activity is developmentally appropriate. Interval training should be introduced within the context of the relay. Teams of *no more than four* should be formed. This structure will cut down on waiting time which is very important. Teams of two or three may also be tried.
2. With four students per relay team, a 1:3 work:rest ratio is created. As one team

member covers the relay distance, the other three team members wait their turn. The turning point should not be less than 30–50 yards away. Round trip for each runner would then range from 60–100 yards. Several repetitions of this sequence would provide a fun, challenging form of interval training.

Materials Needed:

- one mile run time for each student
- interval training task sheet
- pencils
- pace clock

Evaluation:

Reviewing students' task sheets following a learning experience will provide the teacher with information relative to their understanding of interval training. Careful attention should be paid to the number of seconds used for both work and recovery phases.

Related Concepts:

- Training must be progressive (V1, P23)

5×8 card sample (front)

NAME: _____	CLASS: _____	PERIOD: _____
ONE MILE RUN TIME _____	220 Yards (Seconds)*	440 Yards (Seconds)**
5:30– 6:00	40–44	80–87
6:01– 6:30	45–49	88–95
6:31– 7:00	50–54	96–103
7:01– 7:30	55–59	104–111
7:31– 8:00	60–64	112–119
8:01– 8:30	65–69	120–127
8:31– 9:00	70–74	128–135
9:01– 9:30	75–79	136–143
9:31–10:00	80–84	144–151
over 10:01	85+	152+

* 220 Yard Intervals: Perform 6–12 repetitions with from 40–60 seconds of walking recovery between each run.

** 440 Yard Intervals: Perform 4–6 repetitions with 60–90 seconds of walking recovery between each run. Monitor Recovery Heart Rate to make sure heart rate returns to below 140 after each work interval. If not, rest longer.

My 220 Yard Interval Training Plan:
1. Suggested time period _____ seconds.
2. Number of repetitions _____.

My 440 Yard Interval Training Plan:
1. Suggested time period _____ seconds.
2. Number of repetitions _____.

5×8 card sample (back)

Perform either your 220 yard *or* your 440 yard training plan. Monitor your recovery heart rate to make sure you adequately recover (HR 140) before beginning the next work interval

_____ yard plan

_____ # of repetitions

1	3	5	7	9	11
work sec.	work sec.	work sec.	work sec.	work sec.	work sec.

2	4	6	8	10	12
recovery sec.	recovery sec.	recovery sec.	recovery sec.	recovery sec.	recovery sec.

Topic: Circuit Training

Circuit training can be very useful in developing and maintaining physical fitness (V1, P69)

Circuit training is often used to structure fitness activities. A series of exercise stations make up the circuit. The objective is to complete the exercises at each station and move on to the next, through the circuit. Circuits may be designed to enhance a particular component of fitness, such as cardiovascular endurance or flexibility, or to foster overall fitness. Circuit training keeps students active, and, if structured properly, can be exciting and fun.

As a result of this learning experience, students will understand the purpose of circuit training, and will be able to design a relevant series of activities for an overall fitness circuit.

Learning Experiences:

A. Circuit Training for Cardiovascular Endurance: "Countdown"

1. Discuss the principle of circuit training. Contrast it with continuous and interval training.
2. In an area about the size of a basketball court, situate five station charts (described below). Each station requires jogging a certain number of laps around the periphery of the station area. After completing the jogging portion of each station assignment, a skill-related activity that enhances cardiorespiratory endurance is performed. These activities are performed on the inside of the station area. Remember, this is not a race; students should work at their own pace.
3. A class roster and a pencil can be placed at each station. Students can check off each station on the roster as they complete it.
4. Divide the class into five even groups for each station. Establish a clockwise rotation so that everyone is moving in the same direction.
5. This circuit can be modified in any number of ways. After jogging at each station, flexibility exercises may be added to create a cardiovascular endurance *and* flexibility circuit.
6. Students should be allowed to change stations as they complete the activities. There may be a bit of overlap but it should not interfere with the activities if the stations are carefully spaced and enough room and equipment provided for each activity.
7. Use upbeat music in the background.
8. As a modification of this activity, have students work in pairs. At each station, one partner jogs first while the other performs the station skill activity. Once both

partners have completed both tasks, they move on to the next station together.
9. As a homework assignment, ask students to think of ideas for circuit training stations. They should be able to indicate if the activity is intended to develop aerobic capacity, strength, or flexibility.

B. Pre-Programmed Circuit Training

If desired, circuit training can be a bit more programmed. Music can be recorded in specific time intervals. For example, music can be recorded for one minute with a five second period of silence. During the music phase, students should be active, while during the silent phase, students should be moving to the next station. Again, establishing a consistent pattern of station rotation will help.

Pre-recorded music frees the teacher to either be involved in the circuit as a participant or to provide instruction. The circuit activities should be carefully explained and demonstrated prior to beginning the active part of the lesson.

Materials Needed:

- music
- station markers
- pencils
- station charts: (make your own or use "Countdown")
- "Check-Off Sheets: Circuit Training"

Evaluation:

Students should always work at their own pace. Evaluation should be based on active involvement, not on the speed at which the circuit can be completed.

Related Concepts:

- Regular exercise should be tailored to personal needs (V1, P81)

Information for Station Charts **Example: "Countdown"**
Station 1: jog 5 laps — jump rope 2 minutes — jog to station 2
Station 2: jog 4 laps — do 50 jumping jacks — jog to station 3
Station 3: jog 3 laps — dribble soccer ball around cones, make a shot on goal, repeat (2 minutes) — jog to station 4
Station 4: jog 2 laps — crab walk 1 minute — jog to station 5
Station 5: jog 1 lap — walk briskly 2 minutes — jog to station 1

Check-Off Sheet: Circuit Training

Class: _____   Period: _____

STATIONS

1.					
2.					
3.					
4.					
5.					
6.					
7.					
8.					
9.					
10.					
11.					
12.					
13.					
14.					
15.					
16.					
17.					
18.					
19.					
20.					
21.					
22.					
23.					
24.					
25.					
26.					
27.					
28.					
29.					
30.					

(POST AT EACH STATION)

Topic: Contraindicated Exercises

Strength training must use correct muscles (preliminary concept)

Not all exercises are good for people. It is important to recognize the exercises which place people in jeopardy of injury. Whenever strength or flexibility exercises are performed, the correct muscles and body positions should be used.

As a result of these learning experiences, the student should:

1. Become aware of both correct and incorrect exercise postures.
2. Be able to perform correctly the exercises in question.

Learning Experiences:

Strength Training

1. Discuss the concepts from the discussion section.
2. Distribute copies of the "Contraindicated Exercise" handout or make one large chart for the gymnasium wall.
3. Demonstrate correct and incorrect forms of each exercise. Explain *why*. Allow students to perform *correct* exercises.

Double Leg Lifts ("six inches")—When an individual raises and lowers the legs while lying flat on the back, there is tremendous stress on the lower back and abdominal muscles. Many believe that abdominal muscles are the main working muscles during this activity when, in fact, the hip flexor muscles are working. Performing bent-knee sit-ups or curl-ups strengthens the abdominal muscles.

Straight Leg Sit-ups—Similar to double leg lifts, the back may arch causing injury. As long as the lower back is in contact with the floor, injury is unlikely. Performing abdominal bent-knee curls or bent-knee sit-ups *keeping the lower back flat* is the safest method for strengthening these muscles.

Deep Knee Bends—This exercise puts tremendous strain on the connective tissue (ligaments) and membranes (synovial membrane) of the knee joint. Any activity (duck waddle, deep knee bend, squat thrust) that requires greater than a 90° bend is contraindicated. As long as the knees are only bent at angles greater than 90° such activities are considered safe.

Hurdle Stretch—Performing any stretching activity where the foot is *outside* of the knee *may* cause injury. The common hurdler stretch places considerable stress on the knee joint. The ligaments of the knee may be stretched while in this position. Instead the foot should be pulled in toward the groin area.

Standing Toe Touches—A very common exercise to stretch the hamstring (posterior thigh) muscles is a standing toe touch. This exercise may cause low back strain. Performing the same movement from a sitting position is preferred.

Neck Circles: To protect the cervical vertebra, do not perform neck circles. Neck circles are passive exercises in that the momentum created by the movement creates the motion and little actual stretching is occurring. Instead, the neck should be slowly and deliberately moved forward and to both sides. The hand may be used if only gentle pressure is used to assist in the stretch.

Materials Needed:

● "Contraindicated Exercises" handout (or wall chart)

Evaluation:

Proper stretching and strengthening exercises are important. Students should be observed *carefully* while learning proper techniques. Set students up in pairs to learn to monitor each other. Forming bad habits may lead to unnecessary injury.

Related Concepts:

● Flexibility is necessary for all movement (V1, P33)

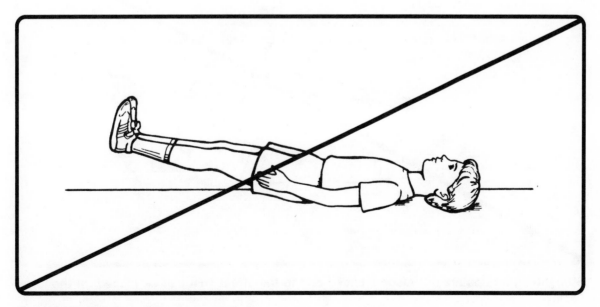

Double leg lifts are not recommended.

Performing bent-knee sit-ups keeping the lower back flat is the safest method for strengthening abdominal muscles.

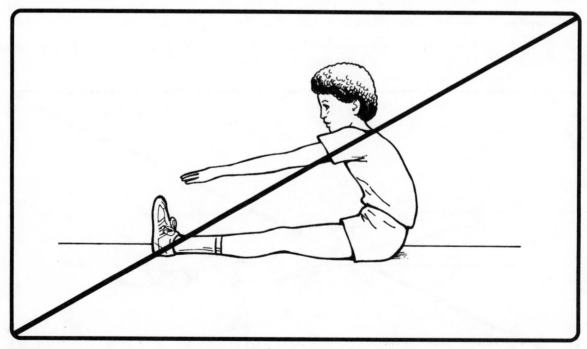

Straight-leg sit-ups are not recommended due to the stress that can be placed on the lower back.

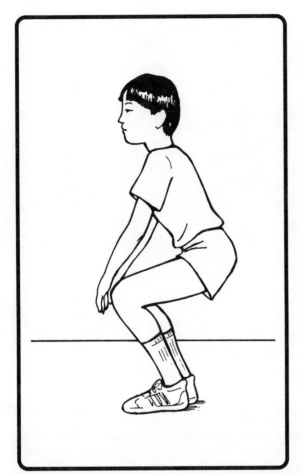 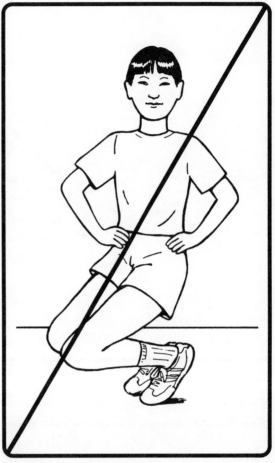

Deep knee bends put tremendous strain on the connective tissue (ligaments) and membranes (synovial membrane) of the knee joint. Instead, a 90° bend is recommended.

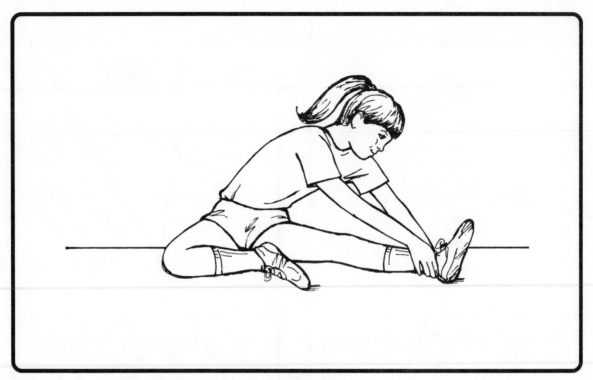

Correct position with foot pulled in toward groin area.

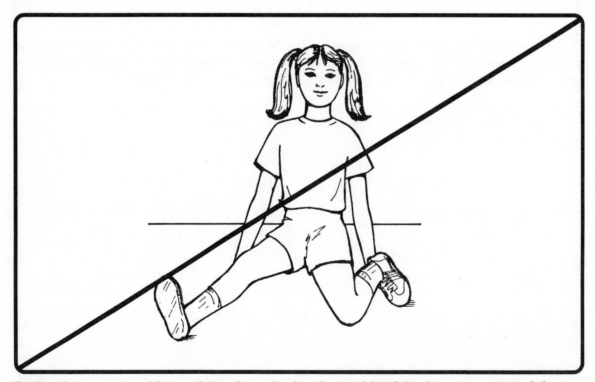

Performing any stretching activity where the foot is outside of the knee may cause injury.

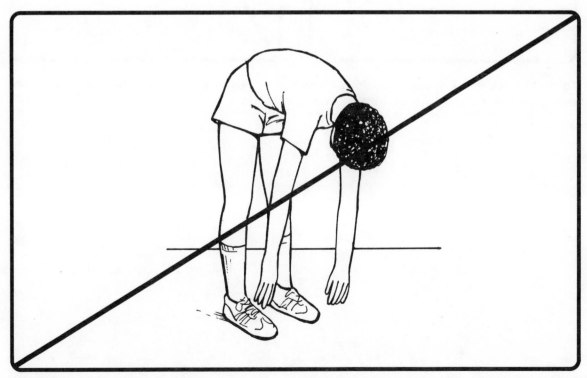

Standing toe touches may cause low back strain. Performing the same movement from a sitting position is preferred.

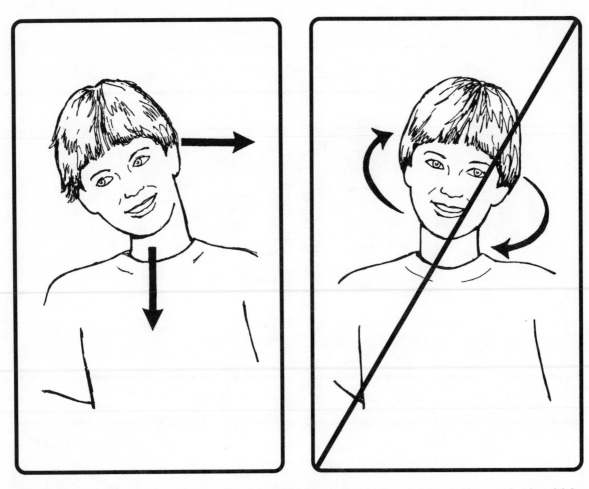

To protect the cervical vertebra, do not perform neck circles. Instead, the neck should be slowly and deliberately moved forward and to both sides.

Topic: Muscular Strength and Endurance

Adequate strength and muscle endurance are necessary in many activities (V1, P2)

Strength is the greatest amount of force a muscle can exert in a single effort. Muscular endurance, on the other hand, involves repeatedly performing moderate to light resistance training with a specific group of muscles. Therefore, strength is best measured by moving a maximal amount of weight while endurance is measured via moving light to moderate weight repetitively.

Most activities require both strength and endurance. Careful selection of activity experiences will help enhance these important components of fitness. As a result of these learning experiences the student will be able to analyze types of muscular strength and endurance required to perform the activities.

Learning Experiences:

A. Analysis of Muscular Strength and Endurance

1. Discuss the concepts from the discussion section.
2. Analyze each game activity according to the muscular strength and muscular endurance necessary to perform adequately.
3. Organize the class for several game-like experiences. Teams should consist of about 5–6 players each.
   a. Game One—Balloon Pass
      1. Teams of about 5 players
      2. Object: To move the balloon from a center toss across a designated goal line. Playing field may be any dimension.
      3. Rules:
         a. The balloon may be tapped with one hand only.
         b. It may not be held or kicked.
         c. It may not be burst intentionally.
      4. Scoring:
         1 point for goal scored
         1 point for the other team if a balloon is burst intentionally.

Analysis of Balloon Pass:

Muscular Endurance	*Muscular Strength*
Legs	Arms
Arms	
Etc.	

  b. *Game Two*—Simple Crab Soccer
  1. Teams of about 5–8 players (smaller groups are better).
  2. Object: To move the soccer ball from a center face off across a designated goal line.
  3. Rules:
     a. The ball may be moved with the feet only.
     b. Obstruction of other players is forbidden.
  4. Scoring: 1 point for goal scored.

Analysis of Simple Crab Soccer:

Muscular Endurance	*Muscular Strength*
Arms/Shoulders/Back	Legs
Abdominal	Arms/Shoulders
Legs/Hips	

  c. *Game Three:* Blast Off!
  1. All students moving around in general space.
  2. *Object:* A countdown is provided (10, 9, 8, . . .). All students must attempt to get *all* body parts suspended off the floor prior to the count of Blast Off! Ropes, parallel bars, climbing nets, wall bars, etc. may be used. If the body is still in contact with the floor on Blast Off!, those students must maneuver (jog) for refueling before re-entering the Blast Off! area.

Analysis of Blast Off!:

Muscular Endurance	*Muscular Strength*
Legs (running)	Arms/Shoulders (hanging and pulling up)
Arms/Shoulders (hanging)	

At the close of the class session, discuss with students the games used above.

B. Muscle Strength/Endurance Ideas

1. Upper Body Strength/Endurance: Negative Pull-ups
   Begin with chin above bar (flexed arm hang position). Gradually lower body (as slowly as possible) and repeat.
2. Tote That Barge
   The activity requires towels and a rope long enough to span the length or width of the gymnasium. Secure one end of the rope to the wall. Students lie down on their backs on a towel, with the head toward the secured end of the rope. The objective is to move the body along the floor using the rope. Feet should not be used to provide force. (Multiple stations are suggested.)
3. Partner Strength and Endurance
   Set up the learning area in stations. Make a sign for each of 8 stations. Students work in pairs to accomplish each of the following partner activities. Jeff Peterson (Laramie, Wyoming) uses these partner strength and endurance activities.
   a. Shoulder: Wheel Barrows—One partner lies in prone position, with arms fully extended and legs spread apart. Partner grabs the legs at the knees, lifting them from the floor. Students move slowly forward for a specific distance. Student in down position should set the pace. *More difficult—grab partner's ankles.

b. Arm: Partner Pull-Ups—One partner lies in the supine position with feet together; the other stands erect, astride the partner, facing partner. Hands are grasped, keeping arms fully extended. Student in down position pulls up and returns to starting position. Student in up position should keep arms straight. Standing partner is also performing isometric work with arm and back muscles.

c. Back: Caterpillars—Partners in crawling position (hands and knees), one behind the other. Person in front places feet on shoulders of partner. Together they attempt to walk forward, slowly at first to coordinate movements.

d. Abdomen: Partner Toe Touches—Partners lie head to head in the supine position. Arms are clasped in hand-wrist grip. Partners bend their knees and then raise their legs overhead until toes touch, then return to starting position. Increasing the distance between head also will help lower back flexibility. Care should be taken not to put too much pressure on the back of the neck.

e. Thigh: Partner Hops—Partners stand facing each other approximately three feet apart. The left leg is extended forward and grasped at the ankle by partner. Partners hop simultaneously and travel in a circle. Try it on the other foot. Partner Hops is also good for flexibility and should be performed after proper warm-up.

f. Knee: Partner Squats—Partners stand facing with right hands clasped together. One student slowly bends one knee, opposite knee is held straight and off the ground. Student continues to squat approaching a half squat (no less than 90°). Hold position for a 5 count. Return to standing position. Try it on the opposite foot, then give partner a try.

g. Leg: Teeter Totters—Partners stand facing each other 12 to 15 inches apart with hands clasped. First partner squats so that knees form a half squat while partner remains standing. Partner returns to standing position and partner #2 takes turn. Standing partner should be assisting while partner is performing the half squat.

Materials Needed:
- balloons
- soccer ball
- apparatus for total body suspension (ropes, wall bars, climbing bars, etc. Hopefully, enough so all students can participate at once.)
- long tug-of-war type rope
- bath towels
- station markers and signs

Evaluation:
Formal testing of strength and endurance may not be warranted at this level. However, informal testing may be done in order to assist individual student improvement. These results may be shared privately with students for their understanding and should avoid being compared to local, state, or national norms. The teacher should carefully observe students to determine their success at these strength/endurance activities. Specific strength and endurance development activities should be provided if necessary. Again, activities must be planned so that strength and endurance are a part of each lesson.

Related Concepts:
- Training for anaerobic power differs from training for anaerobic endurance (V1, P16)

Topic: Stretching for Flexibility

Static stretching improves flexibility (V1, P33)

As mentioned in the Learning Experience entitled "Warming Up for Exercise," stretching for flexibility is best done following vigorous aerobic activity. Time must be taken in order to develop and maintain flexibility. A static, sustained method of stretching is most effective. Each stretch should be held no less than 15 seconds and preferably 30 seconds or longer. All stretching exercises should be performed with the body in proper alignment. Hyperextension at any joint or combination of joints can result in injury. Ballistic stretching generally should be avoided.

Flexibility does not occur when muscles are exercised. On the contrary, when muscles are exercised, as in jogging, they and their associated connective tissues tend to shorten or become less flexible. In order to maintain or improve flexibility and range of motion, time following exercise must be spent stretching the muscles utilized.

Learning Experiences:

Measuring Flexibility

1. Discuss the concepts from the discussion section.
2. Demonstrate the flexibility tests on the "General Flexibility Task Sheet." Arrange the teaching area into learning centers with the appropriate testing equipment.
3. Allow students to select partners. Provide each student with a "Task Sheet" and pencil.
4. Following the activity, discuss each measurement taken and provide developmentally appropriate flexibility exercises for maintaining and improving flexibility.

Materials Needed:

- tape measure—at least 1 per student group
- twelve inch ruler—at least 1 per group
- "General Flexibility Task Sheets" and pencils

Evaluation:

This is a form of self and peer evaluation. Though these measures are not absolutely accurate they provide the student with a general idea of flexibility strengths and weaknesses. The teacher may use the information to help determine specific student flexibility needs.

Name: _____ Partner: _____

General Flexibility Task Sheet

The scale used in these tests is a 1–5 point scale with 5 being the best score. Circle the score that you receive on each test. The purpose of this test is to give you an *idea* of how flexible you are. It is *not an accurate measure.*

1. *ACHILLES TENDON (HEEL)*
   Test: Sit in "L"—seat position. Flex ankle bringing the toes toward the knees as far as possible. Have partners judge the angle of the feet to the floor using cardboard with painted and labeled angles.

Over 100 degrees	5
90–100 degrees	4
80–90 degrees	3
70–80 degrees	2
Under 70 degrees	1

2. *HAMSTRINGS*
   Test: Lie on back. Lift one leg up toward ceiling keeping the other leg straight and on the floor until lifted leg feels stretched. Partners judge angle of lifted leg to floor.

Over 100 degrees	5
90–100 degrees	4
80–90 degrees	3
70–80 degrees	2
Under 70 degrees	1

3. *TRUNK FLEXORS (SPINE AND HAMSTRINGS)*
   Test: Long sitting position with heels about 18 inches apart and hands at neck—keep legs straight. Bend forward toward the floor. Measure from the forehead to the floor.

Less than 8 inches	5
8–10 inches	4
10–12 inches	3
12–14 inches	2
Over 14 inches	1

4. *SHOULDER GIRDLE FLEXIBILITY*
   Test: Stand and place right arm behind head. Reach as far downward as possible toward the scapula with palm against the back. Reach upward as far as possible with left arm with palm outward.

Fingers cover the wrist	5
Fingers cover the palm	4
Fingers cover	3
Fingers touch	2
Fingers do not touch	1

5. *UPPER BACK EXTENSORS*
   Test: Lie on stomach, forehead on the floor and grasp a 12 inch ruler at either end. Keep arms straight and *forehead on the floor* and lift arms as high as possible. Measure from the center of the ruler to the floor.

12 inches and more	5
10–12 inches	4
8–10 inches	3
4–8 inches	2
4 inches and less	1

Topic: Warming Up for Physical Activity

Preparing muscles, tendons and ligaments for exercise makes them less prone to injury (preliminary concept)

Warming up for activity is important. Blood flow is increased, carrying more oxygen to the muscles, and waste materials are eliminated from the working muscles faster. Heart rate, blood pressure, muscle temperature, and respiration are increased also. An adequate warm-up prepares the body for vigorous exercise and makes the body less susceptible to injury. This phase of the exercise workout should not take the place of stretching to improve flexibility. Stretching to enhance flexibility can be performed at any time, but immediately following exercise is a good choice.

As a result of these learning experiences, the student will:

1. Understand the reasons for warming up prior to vigorous exercise.
2. Be able to perform low intensity activities prior to vigorous exercise.
3. Be self-directed while warming up for class.

Learning Experiences:

A. *Warming up for Exercise*

1. Discuss the concepts from the discussion section.
2. *Teach* proper methods for warming up:
   a. Jog slowly for a couple of minutes prior to stretching.
   b. When stretching, do static stretching.
   c. Warm up the muscles that will be used during the vigorous phase of the lesson.
   d. Teach proper breathing—*do not* hold breath while stretching. Slow, rhythmic breathing should be possible.
   e. Stretching is not a contest. Emphasis should be on the "feel" of the stretch and not on the degree of flexibility.
   f. "No pain, no gain" is a dangerous myth. One should not feel pain during stretching activities. If so, cease doing the movement or relax the position until no pain is felt.
3. Look for proper form and assist students when necessary.
4. The slow jog prior to stretching may be used to teach a concept about the circulation of blood. Gather all students in a close group. As the "heart" pumps, they jog slowly around the area and return. The "heart" pumps again and they travel about the area again. This activity can be varied and made a bit more descriptive. As the "heart" pumps students can travel pathways denoting various parts of the circulatory system. The gym should be set up to depict the pathway.

B. Wheel of Fitness

1. Often time is wasted when students first come into the gym. Students can easily accept the responsibility of warming up for activity.
2. Make sure students understand the procedure for warming up and participate in light jogging prior to performing stretching exercises. Also, be sure students understand the names of all the exercises. To assist with this, use wall charts with diagrams.
3. Several different warmup routines can be displayed on the gymnasium wall. Each routine should have a number. As students enter the gym, they spin the Wheel of Fitness to determine their warm-up routine for the day. Routines should be rather general and use the total body. The teacher can add stretches which may be important for the day's lesson.
4. Multiple wheels may be provided to avoid waiting.

Note: This idea may be adapted for use with other concepts as well.

Materials Needed:

- pace clock
- "Wheel of Fitness"
- Warm-up routine charts

Evaluation:

The teacher should check for proper stretching technique and assist students when necessary.

Related Concepts:

- Low back pain can be lessened by strong abdominal muscles (V1, P79)
- Gradual increase in activity level lessens muscle soreness (V1, P73)
- Warm-up can help maximize anaerobic performances (V1, P48)

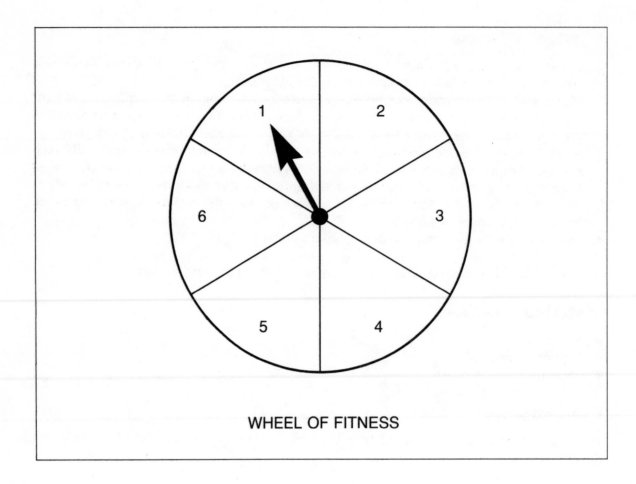

WHEEL OF FITNESS

Topic: Cooling Down After Physical Activity

Gradually tapering off exercise helps the body return to normal after a vigorous workout (preliminary concept)

A cool down phase should follow vigorous activity. The student should continue moving for about 5 minutes in order to adequately recover. The cooling down phase is to allow the muscles in the arms and legs to help pump the blood back to the heart. Venous blood return to the heart is facilitated by the contraction of muscles. If this is not done, blood may pool in the muscles and cause decreased blood flow to other body parts. Dizziness may result from this phenomenon; individuals may actually pass out. Therefore, it is important to keep moving after exercise!

As a result of this learning experience, the student will:

1. Properly cool down after vigorous activity.
2. Understand the reasons for a cool down phase.
3. Determine their recovery heart rate following exercise.

Learning Experiences:

Recovery Heart Rate

1. Discuss the concepts from the discussion section.
2. Instruct the students to continue moving after exercise. They should continue using the predominant muscles used during the activity (e.g. if doing weightbearing activities, walk to cool down; if swimming or cycling, continue at a very low intensity).
3. After five minutes of cool down activity, the students should monitor their recovery heart rate. Most students should be 120 beats per minute or lower. Many students will be 100 beats per minute or lower. Ideally, students should reach 100 beats per minute or less before considering themselves recovered.
4. During the five minute recovery time students can move around the gymnasium collecting the small equipment used in class. This helps the teacher with management chores.
5. Following the cool down phase, stretching for flexibility should be done.

Materials Needed:

- stopwatch or pace clock
- paper or cards to record recovery heart rate
- pencils

Evaluation:

Spot check students' recovery heart rates. Randomly select students or choose students who may have had difficulty monitoring heart rate.

Related Concepts:

- Gradual increase in activity level lessens muscle soreness (V1, P73)

Topic: Body Composition

Inactivity more than food intake contributes to obesity (V1, P55)

The most consistent cause of obesity is lack of physical activity. In fact, obese individuals tend to move around minimally during the day and do not necessarily eat more than leaner individuals. Because physical activity is a critical component in fat loss programs, it is important for the individual to:

1. enjoy the activity
2. participate as frequently as possible (at least 5 times per week, preferably more)

The program should include prolonged aerobic activities of low to moderate intensity that will result in the expenditure of at least 300 kilocalories per session.

Even though weight bearing forms of exercise are preferred because of greater caloric demand, often weight bearing activities such as jogging cause tremendous stress on the ankles, knees, and hips. Such stress often results in injury, at which point no activity occurs. Other aerobic activity choices would include swimming and stationary bicycling. If these are not possible, walking would be a better choice than jogging.

The number of kilocalories expended during activity is determined primarily by the (1) intensity of the activity and (2) body weight of the exerciser. The greater the intensity of the activity, the more calories expended while exercising. Likewise, the greater the body weight, the more energy required to move that weight.

As a result of these learning experiences, the student will:

1. Understand the relationship between physical activity and caloric expenditure.
2. Understand the relative effect of body weight on energy expenditure.
3. Be able to determine preferred activity choices.

Learning Experiences:

A. *Physical Activity and Energy Expenditure*

1. Discuss the concepts from the discussion section.
2. Set up the gymnasium into six activity centers:
- basketball
- calisthenics
- aerobic dancing
- jogging
- soccer
- walking

   If space is limited, select from these six activities, or use other aerobic type activities.
3. Students should select one activity and remain active for at least 20 minutes. Each activity must have specific instructions and necessary equipment. For example, if aerobic dance is used, either a "teacher" must lead a routine or a videocassette player and monitor can be used to play a pre-recorded tape. The calisthenics station should have a chart of exercises to perform.
4. The student should participate in a chosen activity for a specified period of time and then complete the Activity Task Card.

B. *Determining Activity Preferences*

Students can complete the "Activity Preference Sheet" which will help them determine the activities for which they are best suited.

Materials Needed:

A.

- basketballs
- exercise charts
- aerobic dance video—or "teacher" to lead routine
- pace clock
- soccer ball
- "Activity Task Card"
- pencils

B.

- "Activity Preference Sheet"

Evaluation:

Both Learning Experiences may be evaluated based upon the student's completion of each task sheet.

Related Concepts:

- Exercise helps control obesity (V1, P53)
- Prolonged aerobic activities reduce obesity (V1, P53)
- Exercise may help prevent heart disease and stroke (V1, P65)
- Regular exercise should be tailored to personal needs (V1, P81)

ACTIVITY TASK CARD

(5×8 Index Card—Front)

CALORIES USED *PER MINUTE*
(choose one closest to your weight)

ACTIVITY	75 lb.	100 lb.
I. Basketball		
A. Half Court	2.1	2.8
B. Full Court	4.5	6.0
II. Calisthenics	2.5	3.3
III. Dancing		
A. Moderate	2.25	3.0
B. Vigorous	4.13	5.5
IV. Jogging		
A. 5 mph	5.25	7.0
B. 5.5 mph	5.63	7.5
C. 6 mph	6.0	8.0
V. Soccer	4.73	6.3
VI. Walking		
A. 2 mph	1.5	2.0
B. 3 mph	2.1	2.8
C. 4 mph	3.15	4.2

(5×8 Index Card—Back)

NAME _____ Class _____ Period _____

1. Choose one activity and perform for 20 minutes or more in the designated activity area.

2. Complete the chart below.

_____	_____ ×	_____ =	_____
ACTIVITY	# of Minutes	CALORIES PER MINUTE	TOTAL CALORIES USED

ACTIVITY PREFERENCE SHEET

NAME: _____   CLASS: _____   PERIOD: _____

Check (✔) the categories which apply to each activity.

ACTIVITY	I LIKE	I CAN DO ALONE	NOT EXPENSIVE	I CAN DO AWAY FROM SCHOOL
Walking				
Bicycling				
Tennis				
Frisbee				
Skate Boarding				
Roller Skating				
Jogging				
Swimming				
Soccer				
Mowing the Lawn				
Basketball				
Tag				
Rope Jumping				

Topic: Assessment of Body Composition

Exercise helps control obesity (V1, P53)

It is estimated that approximately one-third of Americans are too fat. Often we refer to this problem as being "overweight." Actually, being "overfat" is the correct terminology for the problem. Many individuals, particularly athletes, may be considered "overweight" because their weight is higher than average. This is not a problem if the extra weight is muscle weight. On the other hand, when excessive weight is due to an over-abundance of body fat, a problem does exist—being overfat.

Exercise tends to tone muscle tissue. Since muscle weighs about 2.5 times more than fat, it is possible to lose fat and actually gain weight. This concept is often difficult for students to understand, though very critical nonetheless. Often individuals perceive that exercise is making them "fatter" because they rely upon their body weight for information as opposed to determining their body fatness.

A common method of estimating body fatness is through the use of skinfold calipers. It is estimated that approximately 40% of the body's fat is stored under the skin. Therefore, formulas have been developed which help us estimate total body fatness relative to the thickness of skinfold measures in specific regions of the body.

As a result of this learning experience the student will be able to determine and understand their estimated percent of body fat.

Learning Experiences:

Estimating Percent of Body Fat

1. Discuss the concepts from the discussion section.
2. Using the AAHPERD Health Related Fitness Test's description of the skinfold test, get both triceps and subscapular measurements on each student. A station set-up is recommended with other or related activities so that time is not wasted.
3. Provide students with a copy of the "Skinfold Assessment Handout." Have them determine their total skinfold measurement (triceps + subscapular) in millimeters (mm) and locate their total across the top of the grid. Next, they can find their estimated percent body fat across the bottom of the grid.

Materials Needed:

- skinfold calipers
- "Skinfold Assessment Handout"
- pencils

● AAHPERD Health Related Fitness Test

Evaluation:

Determine estimated percent body fat for each student—*no grade should be given.* If too fat, help student set up a prudent weight loss program including diet and exercise or refer student to a concerned school consultant.

References:

Lohman, Tim G. "Skinfolds and the AAHPERD Health Related Fitness Test." Paper presented at the AAHPERD National Convention, Cincinnati, Ohio, April 9–13, 1986.

Related Concepts:

● Inactivity more than food intake contributes to obesity (V1, P55)
● Prolonged aerobic activities reduce obesity (V1, P53)

SKINFOLD ASSESSMENT HANDOUT

Name: _____   Date: _____

BOYS

Skinfold
Total in
mm   5   10   15   20   25   30   35   40   45   50

```
XXXXXXXXXXXXXXXXX
XXXXXXXXXXXXXXXX
```

% FAT   6%   13%   20%
                        OPTIMAL
         LOW FAT   RANGE   HIGH FAT

GIRLS

Skinfold
Total in
mm   5   10   15   20   25   30   35   40   45   50

```
XXXXXXXXXXXXXXXXXXXXX
XXXXXXXXXXXXXXXXXXXXX
```

% FAT   12%   22%   26%   30%
                        OPTIMAL
         LOW FAT   RANGE   HIGH FAT

From Lohman, Tim G. "Skinfolds and the AAHPERD Health Related Fitness Test." Paper presented at the AAHPERD National Convention, Cincinnati, Ohio, April 9–13, 1986.

Topic: Fitness Testing

Performances can be compared with past self-performance or with others of the same age and sex (V3, P55)

Fitness testing is important only to the degree that it complements your program. Testing for the sake of testing has little merit in fitness *education* if our goal is to empower our students with appropriate knowledge and ability to facilitate their growth toward self-management. The testing program should reflect the program goals. When students are tested on fitness items it should give them a message about *what* is important and *why*. It does not make sense to test students' cardiovascular ability if the program does not provide consistent and appropriate experiences to help them improve. When something is tested, its relative importance becomes known to students, but inconsistent messages are sent if no follow-up occurs in the program.

We should spend time preparing students for the tests we choose to administer. For example, prior to testing students' cardiovascular endurance (e.g. the one mile run) students should be involved for about one month in progressive aerobic experiences (fitness games, skill development activities with an endurance component, etc.) We sabotage our best intentions when we test students before they are physically ready to perform well. The same holds true when testing other dynamic fitness measures (e.g. other endurance runs, sit-ups, pull-ups, push-ups, etc.)

As a result of these learning experiences, the student should:

1. Be able to complete satisfactorily selected fitness test items.
2. Understand *what* the test measures and *why* it is important.
3. Demonstrate ability and responsibility for self-testing.

Learning Experiences:

Ideas for Fitness Testing

1. Explain each test item relative to *what* is being tested and *why*. Refer to the *AAHPERD Health Related Fitness Manual* or other appropriate resources.
2. Organize the learning environment according to suggestions presented for each idea.
3. Provide "Individual Fitness Data Cards."
   a. Setting up a fitness testing circuit can accomplish several objectives. First, all students are actively involved while waiting to be tested. Second, several testing items can be included in the circuit. For example, percent body fat can be taken at one station while a trained student assistant (teacher aide, or parent) administers the sit and reach test at another. In fact, if students are taught to administer these

tests, partners may work together to test each other. Some teachers may have difficulty with this concept. However, if we are trying to teach the process of acquiring active lifestyles and want our students to become self-managers, placing less emphasis on absolutely accurate scores and more emphasis on self-edification, this approach has merit. Fitness testing is for the students, not for the grade books.

b. Testing students' cardiovascular fitness often presents a motivational dilemma. Although most cardiovascular activities such as fitness games or aerobic tag, are a lot of fun, simply running laps around a track can be quite boring.

1. Using consecutively numbered popsicle sticks (or 3×5 index cards) give one to each student at the completion of each lap of the track (if on a 440 yard track, four laps equal one mile). At the end of four laps each student should have four popsicle sticks (or 3×5 cards). A separate container could contain a duplicate of all numbers. One or two "winning" numbers are drawn from the container. Small prizes could be awarded or some special privilege granted. [Variation: Create a wheel of numbers and spin the dial to determine lucky numbers.] This method helps the teacher to track the number of laps run by each student and also gives the fastest and slowest runners an equal chance to have their number drawn.

2. The AAHPERD Health Related Fitness Test provides norms for 9-minute, 12-minute, one mile, and 1.5 mile runs. Though each test is appropriate for assessing cardiovascular fitness, the distance runs seem to be easier for students to understand conceptually. When students are asked to run four laps of the track as quickly as they can, it is possible to think about such a distance. However, if students are asked to cover as much distance as possible in 12 minutes, unless they have previous practice, it is more difficult to understand. Regardless of the test used, previous conditioning is necessary (preferably within a fun context) and the tests should be understood conceptually by the student.

3. Have students remain active for 30 consecutive minutes of activity in their target heart rate range. Performing aerobic routines, jogging, and swimming would all be logical activities for this test. Heart rate should be monitored at the end of 30 minutes and perhaps halfway through the activity. This could be simply a competency test (completing 30 minutes or not) or the teacher may wish to require a minimum distance in jogging or swimming for *each student* based upon previous data. Again, self-testing should always be encouraged.

Comment: Fitness test scores should not be used for grading.

Materials Needed:

- "Individual Fitness Data Cards" and pencils
- equipment for fitness testing circuit activities
- skinfold calipers and appropriate graphs and norms
- sit and reach box
- popsicle sticks or 3×5 index cards, numbered—two sets
- stopwatch or pace clock
- small fitness related prizes

Evaluation:

Testing provides a system for evaluation. Again, fitness test scores should *not* be used for determining grades. Rather students may receive credit for completing all tests or for improvement on tests. Teachers must encourage *participation* in the testing phase of their programs and use the information prudently and positively. Giving grades for fitness performance is rewarding the results and not the idea that participation is most important.

Related Concepts:

- Static stretching improves flexibility (V1, P33)
- Aerobic endurance improves maximal oxygen uptake (V1, P28)
- Aerobic endurance is tested by speed or distance in a given time frame (V1, P25)

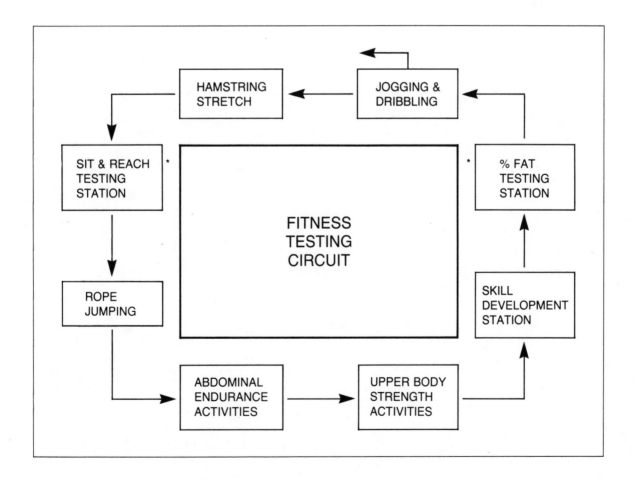

*During fitness testing, these are the locations for the teacher and the teacher's aide.

SAMPLE INDIVIDUAL FITNESS DATA CARD

Name: _____ Grade: _____ Period: _____
        Last   First

Gender: _____   Age: _____

Height: _____ in.   Weight: _____ lbs.

% FAT   _____ _____ _____   RHR= _____   THR= _____ *

SIT UPS   _____ _____ _____   MHR= 220−AGE= _____

SIT & REACH   _____ _____ _____   THR= .75(MHR−RHR)+RHR*

_____ RUN _____ _____ _____   5 minute recovery HR= _____

PUSH-UPS   _____ _____ _____   _____

GOALS: 1.
          2.
          3.

Topic: Integrating Aerobic Fitness and Skill Development

Basic skills are fundamental to successful participation (V6, P21)

Skill development and aerobic fitness may occur simultaneously. As basic locomotor and manipulative skills become easy, activities which involve both motor skills and fitness abilities are appropriate. Many games, lead-up activities, and sports not only require skill but also demand aerobic fitness. Activities such as soccer and team handball are good examples. However, most activities can be modified to enhance skill and aerobic capacity. Games that require a lot of standing and waiting are not good choices to improve skill or aerobic fitness.

As a result of this experience the student will:

1. Be able to work on skill development as well as aerobic fitness.
2. Understand that certain activities enhance both skill and aerobic fitness.

Learning Experiences:

Enhancing Aerobic Fitness in a Volleyball Lesson

Describe the game of Queen's Court Volleyball.

Game Description (Vicky Kmetz—Cheyenne, Wyoming)
Set up the gym with two or more volleyball courts (they do not have to be regulation size). Each team should consist of three or four players. Two teams are on each court while extra teams "actively" wait (jog in place; pursue loose ball). Very little active waiting is needed if play proceeds as it should and several courts are used. Two balls are used on each court—one in play and one with the waiting team.

One team (serving team) serves the ball while the receiving team (Queen's team) attempts to return the ball. If the Queen's team is unsuccessful they run off the court and become a waiting team. The serving team runs under the net to the Queen's court (receiving court) and the waiting team *with the ball* becomes the serving team and serves the ball. If the Queen's team returns the ball and the serving team misses, the serving team runs off the court and the waiting team with the ball becomes the new serving team. *Scoring can only occur when a team is on the Queen's Court* at which time one point is rewarded for every successful volley. The ball may be hit an unlimited number of times before crossing the net. Waiting teams must pursue loose balls in order to gain a chance to play.

Continuous motion should be stressed—the game is very active but when waiting, students should jog.

NOTE: The serving team does *not* have to wait for the Queen's team to pass under the net prior to serving. This keeps players on their toes and also adds to the pace of the game.

Scoring Method:
Method 1—First team to reach 10 points.
Method 2—Set a time limit (20 minutes) the team with the most points wins.

Materials Needed:

● at least two volleyball nets
● at least 4 volleyballs (2 per court)

Evaluation:

Both skill and fitness may be evaluated. This game provides time for using volleyball skill checklists. Also, the teacher should observe for continuous activity relative to aerobic demand.

Related Concepts:

● Sports and games allow opportunities to evaluate personal attributes (V6, P53)
● Physical activity and exercise may improve appearance (V6, P20)

Topic: Personalizing A Fitness Program

Regular exercise should be tailored to personal needs (V1, P81)

The pursuit of physical fitness requires personal commitment and an understanding of oneself relative to likes and dislikes. The ultimate goal of a fitness program is long term adherence to an active lifestyle. Many different factors influence the potential for sustained fitness. Among these are self-motivation, social needs, types of exercise that are enjoyable, current fitness level, and so on. In order to experience the joy and satisfaction being physically fit can bring, establishing a level of personal awareness is important. Beyond that, personal information can help with the planning of your fitness program.

As a result of this learning experience, the student will identify personal likes and dislikes relative to exercise, and will provide important personal information which will be useful in program planning and individual exercise prescription.

Learning Experiences:

Preliminary Screening

1. Discuss the concepts of personal needs and committment to a fitness program. Include a discussion of personal goals and realistic goal setting.
2. Administer the "Preliminary Screening Instrument" to students. Make necessary adaptations for your individual situation.

Materials Needed:

- "Preliminary Screening Instrument" and pencils

Evaluation:

The information gained from the "Preliminary Screening Instrument" is very helpful not only in individualizing instructions, but also as a form of program evaluation. Fitness programs must be personalized in order for students to gain self-awareness and ultimately to become self-managers of their own fitness pursuits.

Related Concepts:

- Personal meaning of movement experience contributes to satisfaction (V5, P42)
- Individual satisfaction is a motivating factor for participation (V5, P25)

Regular exercise should be tailored to personal needs.

photo courtesy of Greg Merhar

PRELIMINARY SCREENING INSTRUMENT

Name: _____ Age: _____ Class: _____

Gender: _____ (Male or Female)

1. How do you feel about fitness activities like jogging, swimming, aerobic dance?
   _____ Like   _____ Dislike

2. Considering all the physical activities you participate in, how do you compare with your friends:
   _____ Not as active
   _____ About the same
   _____ More active

3. Do you like to play games after school? _____Yes   _____No

   What games do you play? _____

   _____

4. Do you like to participate in physical activities alone or with friends/family?
   _____ Alone
   _____ With others

5. If you could choose *one main* fitness activity, what would it be?

   ____ Jogging   ____ Swimming   ____ Bicycling   ____ Aerobics   ____ Other

   ____ Jumping Rope   ____ Fitness games (like soccer, tag games)   _____
                                                                     What?

6. How many days per week do you get at least 30 minutes of continuous exercise?
   _____

7. Please fill in the following information if you know it. Your teacher can help you with fitness scores.

   ____ Weight   ____ 1 Mile Run   ____ Sit and Reach

   ____ Height   ____ Situps   ____ % Fat

   ____ Target Heart Rate   ____ Resting Heart Rate

8. What are some of the activities you would like to do in physical education?

   _____

AN INVITATION
FROM AAHPERD/NASPE

The American Alliance for Health, Physical Education, Recreation, and Dance, NASPE, and the many *Basic Stuff* authors cordially invite *you* to become a participating author and to design or share current learning experiences with other professionals throughout the United States. Using the format guidelines on the following page, please complete your Learning Experience, indicate your name and professional affiliation, and mail it to:

Acquisitions Editor
Basic Stuff Project
AAHPERD
1900 Association Drive
Reston, VA 22091

As soon as we have an adequate number of Learning Experiences, we will publish them under a title such as *The Best of Basic Stuff*.

Topic:_____

Grade Level: ☐ K–3   ☐ 4–8   ☐ 9–12

Goal: ☐ Personal Fitness   ☐ Skillful Moving   ☐ Joy, Pleasure, & Satisfaction

Concept:_____

_____ volume _____ page _____

Discussion *(introduction to concept, definitions, relationships, purposes, outcomes, etc.):*_____

_____

_____

_____

Conceptual Focus *(What are the main points of this topic?):*

1. _____

_____

2. _____

_____

3. _____

_____

Learning Experiences *(includes tasks, classwork, labs, homework, etc.—small tables, charts, and worksheets included here):*

1. _____

_____

2. _____

_____

3. _____

_____

Materials Needed:

● _____

● _____

● _____

Evaluation:

1. _____

_____

2. _____

_____

References *(need only if very specific references used or suggested):*

_____

_____

Related Concepts:

● _____ volume _____ page _____

● _____ volume _____ page _____

● _____ volume _____ page _____

Attach additional full page lab experiences, worksheets, take-homes, transparencies, duplicating masters, and other materials

chapter four
Skillful Moving

In many textbooks for elementary school physical education, skill development is a primary goal in the teaching-learning process. Several texts use basically the same terminology with reference to the objectives sought in skill development, that is, the learner should become optimally efficient, effective, and versatile in movement skills. Some texts define these terms while others do not. It is very important that practitioners are aware of this terminology if they are to provide the educational experiences necessary for students to reach these goals. Efficient skill development suggests economy of motion and ease of action. Effective skill development refers to the actual accomplishment of a task, whether it is hitting a target a prescribed number of times or jumping a specified height or distance. Versatility refers to an ability to make adjustments in skill performance within a fraction of a second or over a period of time. Appropriate lesson planning is imperative if each of these objectives of motor skill development is to be met.

Volumes have been written about lesson planning; therefore, any attempts to cover that topic extensively in this limited space would be inappropriate. However, there is one essential aspect of planning a lesson, supported by both research and common sense, that should be incorporated by all physical educators—a lesson must maximize active learning time (ALT). Each student in a class must have as much opportunity to practice the skills to be learned as time and effective organizational procedures will allow. Alternative terms for ALT are "practice time" or "movement time" but, no matter what it is called, without sufficient time to practice, optimal efficiency and effectiveness in skill development will not occur.

There are many reasons why elementary and middle school students should become competent in motor skills. First, there is no better phase in the lives of students when they will have the time needed to spend in skill practice and play. Second, motor skills are long remembered. Hence, a solid skill base developed early in life will be an asset throughout life. For example, if people learn to ride a bicycle at eight years of age, they could experience thirty years or more without being on a bicycle, but after that time still be able to ride successfully. This example suggests the long duration of motor memory.

Motor skill development also is important for peer acceptance. There is no doubt that a highly skilled person has certain social interaction advantages over a person with low skill level ability.

According to Piaget (1954) and Getman (1962), motoric experiences serve as an appropriate process in the development of children. A summary of their findings indicates that early motor experiences are very important in establishing a child's understanding in relation to people, objects, and concepts. In effect, the child learns how to learn and how to relate socially to others through sensorimotor experiences. It becomes obvious, then, that it is not desirable to leave such experiences to chance occurrence. An intelligently planned physical education program can be instrumental in providing these needed experiences.

Finally, if Bloom (1964) is correct in that "ninety percent of a person's habits and attitudes are established by age 12" then it is certainly necessary that positive effective mindsets are established at the elementary and middle school levels. An ability and a desire for skillful participation in activity and a proper attitude toward the maintenance of physical fitness are necessary for the enhancement of a high quality life.

References

Bloom, B. (1964). *Stability and change in human characteristics.* New York: Wiley and Sons.

Getman, G. (1962). *How to develop your child's intelligence.* Luverne, Minnesota: Announcer's Press.

Piaget, J. (1954). *The construction of reality in the child.* New York: New Basic Books.

Topic: Information Processing and Skill Development

Successful motor performance requires input, decision-making, output, and feedback (V3, P3)

Although there may be more to human learning than simple input-output, successful motor skills performance requires that the learner know and be able to apply the following elements of information processing:

1. Pay attention to important aspects of the environment (INPUT).

2. Determine a motor response effort appropriate to the environment (DECISION-MAKING).

3. Execute the movement (OUTPUT).

4. Evaluate all information obtained from the trial and modify the next response (FEEDBACK).

Examples of input include direction of target, distance, and surface resistance of floor on the ball.

Examples of decision-making include the amount of force needed and the idiosyncrasy of yarn ball (e.g., does it typically curve in specific direction?).

In this lesson students will be asked to putt (strike) yarn balls into hula hoops. The basic skill involved is striking. To have the students understand the application of input, decision-making, output, and feedback, have them watch the teacher (or a student) demonstrate the task. The students would then be asked to identify each phase of the information process, and then brainstorm about specific considerations to be included. The teacher should record, on the chalkboard, the information presented by the students so that it may be referred to later in the closing portion of the lesson.

As a result of this learning experience the student should:

1. Be able to identify the four aspects of information processing.
2. Be able to provide relevant content for each aspect of information processing for a skill other than the skill practiced in class (e.g. striking a tennis ball or bowling).

Learning Experiences:

What to look for in learning a skill

1. Discuss the concepts from the discussion section and indicate the objectives of the learning experience (see 1 and 2 above). Specify to the learners that they are to identify important factors relevant to each aspect of information processing as they relate to the task of putting (striking) a yarn ball into a hula hoop.

2. Indicate that previously learned concepts concerning force production and internal and external producers of force are strongly integrated into various aspects of this lesson.

3. Have each student select a partner. Each pair should have two clubs, two yarn balls (tennis ball size preferred) one hula hoop and one numbered pylon or plastic bowling pin. Demonstrate the skill to be performed; then call upon students to identify appropriate content for the four phases of information processing (Input, Decision-Making, Output, and Feedback). When the most important points have been identified (more information can be added later if desired), have each pair practice putting balls into their hula hoop from progressively greater distances

---

HOW TO MAKE A GOLF CLUB OR HOCKEY STICK

Materials

Hardwood dowel rod, ⅝″ × 3′

Garden hose or rubber tubing, ⅝″ (inside diameter)

Roll of electrical or adhesive tape (one roll will be sufficient for at least 12 sticks)

Two flat headed nails, ⅝″

Coat hanger

Directions

1. Cut an 18″ length of the garden hose and slip it approximately 3½″ onto the dowel.

2. Insert a piece of coat hanger wire into the hose so that it butts up against the bottom of the dowel and extends almost to the end of the hose.

3. Bend the hose so that the ends meet on the dowel rod. The hose can be formed at whatever angle is desired.

4. Use two nails to secure hose to dowel. One of the two nails can be used to attach the bottom portion of the hose bent in half to the top portion.

5. Tape should be used to give further support to the hose on the dowel rod.

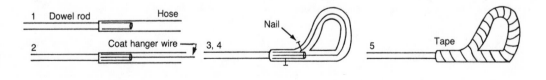

Information Processing Worksheet

Name _____   Grade _____

Lesson Worksheet: What to look for in developing a skill.

Input information: Indicate aspects of the environment that could affect performance.

1

2

3

Decision-Making: What decisions need to be made regarding input in order to have a successful output?

1

2

3

Output: Trial experience(s).

1

2

3

Feedback: Evaluation of what happened in the trial experience(s). Evaluation is feedback that becomes additional input and the process begins again.

1

2

3

starting from five feet. Both students can putt simultaneously at the same target from different directions. To qualify for movement to the next farthest putting distance (10 feet), require the student to reach 80% competency (4 out of 5). After sufficient skill levels have been reached, the teacher should lay numbered arrows on the floor as indicators of places to putt from to start for the next highest numbered hole. The students (in pairs) will then move from hole to hole trying to minimize the number of strokes (putts) it takes to get the ball into each hole. At the conclusion of the lesson the teacher gathers the group around the chalkboard on which the original input from the students was recorded. The students are asked if they have any further suggestions to add to any of the four elements of information processing that they may have discovered during the learning experience.

Materials Needed:

- improvised golf clubs or plastic floor hockey sticks
- hula hoops
- yarn balls (inside) or tennis balls (outside)
- pylons or plastic bowling pins
- arrows to serve as tee markers
- chalkboard and chalk
- copies of "Information Processing Worksheet" and pencils

Evaluation:

Provide an "Information Processing Worksheet" for individual work, or use a chalkboard to have the class as a whole indicate their ability for identifying appropriate content for the Input, Decision-Making, Output, and Feedback aspects of a specific skill chosen by the students or selected by the teacher.

Related Concepts:

- The information processing notion is a way of explaining the acquisition and performance of motor skills (V3, P2)
- Can you identify examples of input, decision-making, output, and feedback? (V3, P3)
- Information processing explains behavior in terms of sequential operations (V3, P6)

Topic: Information Processing and Skill Development

Information processing framework directs investigation of errors (V3, P4)

Decision-making is changing input to output (V3, P10)

Input is information from internal and external sources (V3, P10)

In the preceding learning experience, focus was placed on the information process, that is, the application of input, decision-making, output, and feedback in relation to skill development. In this learning experience special attention will be directed to the use of the information processing framework in the analysis of errors. Teachers will want to be familiar with, and share with their students, errors that might be made at the input, decision-making, output, and feedback phases of information processing in skill development. The "Identifying Errors in Self and Others" form can be used for this purpose.

As a result of this learning experience the student should:

1. Experience some of the errors that might be made in information processing.
2. Be able to identify information processing errors in another person.

Learning Experiences:

Identification of information processing errors in self and others

1. Discuss the concepts from the discussion section and indicate the objectives of this learning experience (1 and 2 above).
2. Indicate to the students that effectiveness in these activities will be enhanced by the application of concepts covered in the lesson on force production.
3. Have each student select a partner. Each pair should have two clubs (plastic floor hockey sticks or improvised golf clubs), two yarn balls (tennis ball size preferred), one hula hoop, one numbered pylon or plastic bowling pin, and one blindfold. Have the students stress the following in striking (putting) the yarn ball into the hula hoop.
   a. Hands on club, right hand below left, (opposite for left handed people) palms of each hand facing in opposite directions.
   b. Knees slightly bent, head over ball and still throughout output phase.
   c. Keep putter blade square to target.
   d. Swing club straight back (limited backswing) with a forward swing that accelerates through impact zone and moves straight forward on line with the target (follow through).

4. One student observes the other via the use of the "Identifying Errors in Self and Others" form. The observers provide verbal input to the partners based on their observations. After an appropriate time the partners reverse roles. Both roles are then repeated but this time with the performer blindfolded.

5. Students practice the above for a few minutes, progressively moving back 5' each time output produces desired results in 4 out of 5 trials.

6. As a culminating activity, students are given the opportunity to play a "round of golf." Set up the equipment so that a sequence of holes forms a "golf course."

7. The close of the lesson should focus on the personal experiences of the student with the use of the information processing framework. The following represent questions that could be asked:

   ● Did you think your awareness and/or use of the information processing framework helped you or your partner in any way? (Have them explain their answers in detail.)

   ● What internal (within the body) feedback did you get when you putted while blindfolded?

   ● Which type of feedback, either from within or external from partner, seemed to be most beneficial to you? (Have responses explained in detail.)

Note: A variety of designs can be organized by the teacher and/or students to make an interesting and creative "golf course."

Materials Needed:

● one club and one yarn ball (tennis ball size) per person
● one blindfold per pair
● pylons
● hula hoops
● "Identifying Errors in Self and Others" forms and pencils

Evaluation:

Conduct discussion at the close of class as described in #7 above. Based on the teacher's subjective evaluation, a determination can be made about whether the lesson's objectives were met.

Related Concepts:

● Feedback directs adjustments in performance (V3, P78)
● Feedback involves movement and outcome information (V3, P78)
● Augmented terminal feedback is most effective (V3, P85)

Identifying Errors In Self and Others

Performer _____   Observer _____

1. Grip: hands on club right hand below left (opposite for left handed persons) with palms facing in opposite directions.

   Comment:

2. Stance: knees slightly bent—head over ball.

   Comment:

3. Address: putter blade square with target.

   | open | square | closed | target |

   Comment:

4. Swing: club swings straight back (limited backswing). Forward swing accelerates through impact zone and moves straight forward to target (follow-through).

   inside
   (toward the body)

   straight ————————————————————————→ target

   outside
   (away from the body)

   ↑ ↑ ↑ ↑
   0 1 2 3

   Does the club head stop at 0, 1, 2, or 3? _____

   Comment:

5. Other errors identified:

   Comment:

Topic: Relating Balance To Skill Effectiveness

Development of body awareness, balance, spatial awareness, and tactile location aids performance (V6, P29)

Announcers of football games will often talk about a player's strength, speed, and agility. If one listens carefully, the comment, "Player X has great balance," also will be heard. The ability to obtain and maintain effective balance is a key element for effortless performance. Highly skilled people make difficult skills appear simple. This would be impossible if the performer had not developed the ability to react instantly to a myriad of balance problems. However, because there is little evidence of a generalized balance ability, it is important that students are given the opportunity to practice many types of balancing experiences.

Concepts concerning balance should be understood by students in order to optimize performance. The learning experiences involve working with the following terms and concepts: center of gravity, base of support, equilibrium, counter-balance, stability, asymmetrical/symmetrical balance, and static and dynamic balance. Instructors may choose to define these terms when introducing the lesson, or to cover the material during the action phase of the lesson.

As a result of the learning experience, the student should be able to provide correct responses to at least 80% of the questions concerning concepts involved in balance.

Learning Experiences:

Physical activities depend upon the ability to balance

1. Discuss the concepts from the discussion and indicate the objective of the learning experience.
2. The organization for this lesson could either be via (small group) station rotation or the class as a whole. The decision would be based on teacher preference and/or availability of equipment. (The following directions, however, will be based on whole class organization.)
3. Provide each student with a pencil and a copy of "Relating Balance to Skill Effectiveness." Have each student select a partner to work with for the period. If possible, have a 4' x 6' mat for each pair. Also, have a 6' to 8' section of wood 2 × 4 or 4 × 4 for each pair.

4. While working on the mats, have all students who have the ability and necessary background experience try the following as the teacher announces them: tip-up, tripod, headstand, handstand (2 hands), handstand (1 hand). When sufficient time has been allotted to try these, have each student independently complete Part I of the handout.

5. Working two people at one time on each beam (wood 2 × 4's or 4 × 4's), have all students who have the ability and necessary background experience try the following as the teacher announces them: squat on beam hands and feet on beam, body in tuck position; hands and feet on beam, body in piked position; stand upright on beam arms at sides, stand on beam using only the balls of the feet with arms stretched in a directly upward position. When completed, have each student independently complete Part II of the handout. (This station may call for heterogeneous grouping if some students cannot complete the tasks.)

6. Have partners stand in a forward-backward stride position with outer edges of right front feet touching (Indian Wrestling). Clasp hands as if shaking hands. On the word "go" attempt to push or pull the other person off balance. If either foot moves that person loses the match. Repeat this five times, then independently complete Part III of the handout.

7. Balance on the beam on the right foot. A) Have persons on the beam move their left legs out to the side as far and as high as possible. B) Move the free foot to the front as high and as far as possible. C) Now, have them move the free foot backward and as high as possible. Have students individually complete Part IV of the handout.

8. The sprint start requires that the sprinter put to practice many principles of balance. Direct the students to establish sprint start positions. On a partner's word "go," practice starts while taking only five or six steps after the start is made. After sufficient time has been given for this activity have the students complete Part V of the handout.

9. As a culminating "fun" and "challenge" conclusion to the activity, see how many partners can do the following: each partner starts from an end of a beam opposite their partner, they then attempt to pass each other to get to the other end without either partner touching the floor with any body part. Secondly, each pair one at a time, adds their beam to make a maze of beams and everyone in the class walks all of the beams in continuous order, trying to minimize the number of times balance is lost.

Materials Needed:

- beams 2 × 4's and 4 × 4's
- mats
- "Relating Balance to Skill Effectiveness" worksheets and pencils

Evaluation:

In the closing phase of this learning experience, the teacher critiques the handout with the students while supplying additional information and answering questions. Students grade their worksheets to determine if an 80% or better comprehension rate was achieved.

References:

Ideas for this learning experience were extracted from materials prepared by Kathy Nelson, University of Wisconsin, LaCrosse.

Related Concepts:

- When forces are counter-balanced by equal and opposite forces, equilibrium is maintained (V2, P42)
- Equilibrium is attained when the center of gravity is over the base of support (V2, P42)
- The center of gravity is the point at which the mass of a body may be considered to be concentrated (V2, P42)
- The base of support of the human body is the area outlined by the supporting body surfaces (V2, P42)
- The greater the stability of an object the more difficult it is to disturb its equilibrium (V2, P42)
- Neutral equilibrium occurs when the moving object's center of gravity remains at the same height (V2, P43)
- Unstable equilibrium causes the object to be more easily unbalanced (V2, P43)
- Stability depends upon the height of the center of gravity, direction and size of the base of support, and the location of the line of gravity over the base (V2, P44)

Relating Balance To Skill Effectiveness

Name _____   Date _____

Part I: Determine the order of difficulty for these stunts based upon the effectiveness of the base of support and height of the center of gravity.

	Base of Support	*Height of Center of Gravity (COG)*	*Difficulty (Rank)*
	Indicate comments and/or diagrams to help describe the base of support	Indicate comments and/or diagrams to help describe the location of the COG	Based on the combined factors of base of support and height of COG (1 = easiest)
A. Tip Up	Example comment: B and C have three point bases, while A and D have two point bases. E has one point base.	Example comment: A has the lowest COG. B has a slightly higher COG and C, D, and E have much higher COG than A.	*Answers:* (2)
B. Tripod			(1)
C. Headstand			(3)
D. Handstand (two hands)			(4)
E. Handstand (one hand)			(5)

Part II: Do the same for stunts A through E below as you did for A-E in Part I.

	Base of Support	*Height of Center of Gravity*	*Difficulty (Rank)*
	Comments and/or diagrams	Comments and/or diagrams	
A. Hands & feet on beam, pike position			(5)
B. Stand on beam on toes, arms stretched directly overhead			(1)
C. Squat on beam, arms out to sides			(3)

continued

Part II continued

D. Hands & feet on beam, tuck position			(4)
E. Stand on beam, feet touching each others arms at sides			(2)

Note: There may be some disagreements about the rank order between items C and A. In the case of C there is less base of support than A, however, the COG height for A is a higher (less stable). In deciding the answer much depends on how much of both feet contact the beam, i.e., all of feet or just balls of feet.

Based on the difficulty ranking in Parts I & II above complete the following:

As a result of experiences you should realize that it is easier to balance in a

_____ position because the _____
(high-*low*)   (higher-*lower*)

the _____
(*COG*-stability)

the greater_____ an object has.
(COG-*stability*)

Part III: In the Indian wrestling activity, the base is largest in the

_____ position, and is narrowest
(*front to back*/side to side)

in the_____ position. Therefore, to
(front to back/*side to side*)

increase stability one should have a_____ base in the direction of the
(small–*large*)

force being applied. In the five attempts at this activity balance was most frequently

lost in the_____ position.
(forward or backward/*side to side*)

Part IV: To balance effectively on the right foot, when the left leg was placed far out to the left side,

you moved your torso to the_____ to establish equilibrium. Your torso
(*right*–left)

moved in that direction in order to maintain the_____ over the
(*COG*–base of support)

_____.
(COG–*base of support*)

continued

Part IV continued

This type of balance, when all body parts are held as still as possible, is called

_____ balance. When forces are counter-balanced by
              dynamic/*static*

equal and opposite forces_____ occurs.
                                    (*equilibrium*–instability)

Part V: In assuming an efficient sprint start position, do you think the position of the sprinter should be: (Circle the correct letter)

1. a. symmetrical
    b. asymmetrical

2. The center of gravity, in relation to base of support, should be:
    a. directly over the base of support
    b. in front of the base of support

3. Is the sprinter's start a stable or unstable position?
    a. stable
    b. unstable

4. Briefly describe why you answered #3 above as you did.

Topic: Body Composition

Body composition influences participation (V6, P6)

Although most students can attain *at least* a minimal skill level in most movement activities, the composition of the body can affect the desire and ability to participate in motor skill experiences. Body composition is defined as the ratio of lean or fat-free weight to fat weight. Most sports, for example, favor persons with lean weight (muscle density) over those with fat weight (fat density). A child with a high degree of body fatness may not participate because of a diminished chance for success due to a negative effect of the body fatness on skill development.

The body composition of an individual is a product of genetic and environmental factors. The learner should understand that taking positive control of environmental factors such as exercise and eating habits can influence the potential for participation in motor performance activities by enhancing the development of skill and the enjoyment of participation.

The student should also understand that appropriate control of eating and exercising can improve personal appearance, enhance acceptance by peers, and improve self concept.

As a result of these learning experiences the student should:

1. Be able to explain positive and negative aspects of body composition with regard to the potential for successful participation in motoric experiences (Learning Experience A).
2. Be able to plan (via P.E. homework or in math class), a frequency, duration, and intensity schedule to permit a 150 pound person to lose 10 pounds using the walking activity experienced in class (Learning Experience B).

Learning Experiences:

A. *Possible effects of body composition on skill performance*

1. Discuss the concepts from the discussion and indicate the objectives of the learning experiences.
2. Indicate that the activities planned are provided to help students assess their levels of performance in each activity. Upon making the assessments they will be asked to determine if a modification in body composition through diet and/or exercise habits could possibly affect future performance in any or all of the activities experienced.
3. Provide each learner with a "Body Composition Worksheet." If necessary, explain what rank order means and detail what is expected of them in the A through D aspects of the form.

4. Arrange five stations emphasizing activities which employ the attributes of dynamic balance, speed, strength, agility, and power. For example, if fitness tests are given they could be used as stations, or self-testing type activities such as long jump, agility shuttle run, or rope climb (vertical or horizontal) could be used.
5. Either at the end of the period or as a homework assignment, have each student complete all aspects of the "Body Composition Worksheet."

B. Effects of diet and exercise on body composition.

1. Share the objectives of the lesson with the students. In addition to covering the salient points made in the discussion, the instructor should provide information regarding caloric balance (i.e., when calories taken in equal calories expended body weight remains stable). The students should be informed that 3500 calories equal one pound. Students should be asked to compute the number of times they would need to complete the day's activity in order to equal the caloric equivalent of some of the food items listed in the "Fast Food Calorie Counter."
2. The teacher should briefly explain the concept of vigorous walking. Under the teacher's leadership the class would then participate in a vigorous walk for 25-30 minutes. The teacher would indicate a close approximation of the caloric burn of the walking activity in which they engaged. In class, at home, or in a math class each student would be asked to answer the following question: If a person with an equal caloric balance (daily caloric input equalled daily caloric output) added a walking activity four times a week, fifty-two weeks a year to his or her daily regimen, how many pounds of fat could be lost?

Materials Needed:

A.

- Equipment for the activity selected by the teacher
- "Body Composition Worksheet," and pencils
- "Activity Task Card" (Body Composition Lesson, Chapter 3)
- "Approximate Calories Burned While Walking"

B.

- "Fast Food Calorie Counter" and pencils

Evaluation:

A. Use the completed worksheet, particularly part C, to determine the students' degree of understanding of the objectives of the lesson.
B. Check the results of students' work regarding their computation concerning the question posed in B2 above.

Related Concepts:

- Appearance is influenced by genetic and environmental factors (V6, P6)
- Mild exercise stress stimulates bone strength and growth (V6, P10)
- Fat content is influenced by eating habits and exercise (V6, P16)
- Physical activity and exercise may improve appearance (V6, P20)
- Prolonged aerobic activities reduce obesity (V1, P53)

BODY COMPOSITION WORKSHEET

Name _____   Grade _____

A. Results (record the appropriate time, distance, height, and data achieved at each station)

  STATIONS:

  1. Dynamic Balance _____

  2. Speed _____

  3. Strength _____

  4. Agility _____

  5. Power _____

B. Rank order according to how successful you feel you were (1 = most successful)

  Station   _____   _____   _____   _____   _____

C. Explain how your body composition helped or hindered your performance at any of the stations.

D. Briefly describe an exercise program which would help to improve your performance at the lowest ranked station.

Approximate Calories Burned while Walking

Food or beverage	Portion	Calories	Minutes Walking
Whole milk	1 cup	160	32
Ice cream	1 cup	255	51
Roast beef	3 oz.	375	75
Hamburger	3 oz.	345	68
Bacon	2 slices	60	12
Boiled chicken	3 oz.	115	23
Green beans	½ cup	15	3
Broccoli	½ cup	25	5
Celery	3 sticks	10	2
Baked potato	1	145	29
French fries	10 pieces	215	43
Apple	1 medium	80	16
Orange juice	½ cup	55	11
Whole wheat bread	1 slice	65	13
Doughnuts	1	165	33
Spaghetti	¾ cup	115	23
Butter or margarine	1 tbsp.	100	20
Mayonnaise	1 tbsp.	100	20
Brownie	1	90	18
Apple pie	1 piece	300	60
Cola	12-oz. can	145	29
Beer	8-oz. glass	100	20
Liquor, 86 proof	1 jigger	105	21
Table wine	1 glass	85	17
Lemonade	½ cup	55	11

UGA Health Services. *University of Georgia Health Services Bulletin.* Athens: UGA Health Services Office, January, 1986.

The Fast Food Calorie Counter

BURGER KING	CALORIES	KENTUCKY FRIED CHICKEN	CALORIES
Cheeseburger	305	2-Piece Dinner—original	595
French Fries	220	2-Piece Dinner—crispy	665
Hamburger	230	3-Piece Dinner—original	980
Chocolate Shake	365	3-Piece Dinner—crispy	1070
Whopper	630		
Whopper, Jr.	285		

McDONALD'S		DAIRY QUEEN	
		Brazier	250
Apple Pie	265	Barbeque	280
Big Mac	557	Cheeseburger	310
Cheeseburger	309	Chili Dog	330
Egg McMuffin	312	Fries	200
Fillet-O-Fish	406	Onion Rings	300
French Fries	215	Big Brazier	510
Hamburger	249	Big Brazier Deluxe	540
Hot Cakes	272	Super Brazier 1/2 Pounder	850
English Muffin	136	Banana Split	580
Sausage	235	Small Cone	110
Quarter Pounder	414	Small Dipped Cone	160
Quarter Pounder/Cheese	521	Small Malt	400
Scrambled Eggs	175	Small Sundae	190
Shake	320	Hot Fudge Brownie	
		Delight Sundae	580
		Parfait	460

PIZZA HUT (thin crust, subtract about 50 calories)		TACO BELL	
1/2 of 13" Cheese Pizza	900		
1/2 of 15" Cheese Pizza	1200	Bean Burrito	345
1/2 of 10" Cheese Pizza	486	Bell Burger	243
1/2 of 10" Beef Pizza	530	Frejohes	231
1/2 of 10" Pepperoni	510	Taco	146
1/2 of 10" Pork	515	Tostado	206
1/2 of 10" Supreme	525		

BASKIN ROBBINS		DUNKIN' DONUTS	
One scoop ice cream	133–146	Plain Donuts	240
One scoop sherbert	139	Yeast Donuts	160
		Fancy Pastries	215
		Munchkins	26

(add 40–50 calories per donut for filling and topping)

By Henry A. Jordon, M.D., Leonard S. Levitz, Ph.D., and Gordon M. Kimbrell, Ph.D., University of Georgia Health Service.

Topic: Creating An Environment For Skill Development

Activities should be appropriate to the developmental level (V6, P3)

It is important that children undergoing growth and developmental changes understand the impact of these phenomena on their motor skill development. It is equally important that both teachers and students understand that the environment can be structured to accommodate the size, strength, and other growth and developmental differences in students. An environment that accommodates the growth and development characteristics of students optimizes the potential for learning motor skills.

Examples of *not* providing an accommodating environment would be having one equipment size for all students in the class or baskets or nets that are the same height for everyone in the class. These non-accommodating environments may negatively affect the learning of some motor skills.

As a result of this learning experience the student should be able to differentiate the growth and/or development characteristics which make various activities appropriate or inappropriate for students.

Learning Experiences:

Learning environment accommodations

1. Discuss the concepts from the discussion section and indicate the objective of the learning experience.
2. During the introduction of the lesson, provide each student with a copy of "Analyzing the Learning Environment" and discuss the expectations indicated on the form.
3. Assign equal numbers of students to four activity stations. If the class is large, double the number of stations.
4. In each of the four stations, two different approaches are provided to accomplish an objective. One approach is more difficult to perform than the other. The difficulty factor is due to the fact one approach requires more growth and/or developmental maturity than the other. The learners are expected to evaluate both their own ability to achieve at each station as well as evaluating peers at each station.
   a. Accommodating growth (height). A variety of growth characteristics, such as height and strength, can have a substantial effect on motor learning and motor performance. This station concerns the need to accommodate for size (height). Provide floor hockey sticks for all students at this station. Divide the teams equally

and have them play a floor hockey game for a specific number of minutes. On each hockey stick the instructor should place a piece of tape a specific number of inches down the handle. All students must hold the stick below the tape even though the location may prove very inefficient for some or maybe all of the students. After playing for several minutes using the restricted grip, then instruct the students to grip the stick at the point at which it is most effective for them.

b. Accommodating growth (body parts-hands). Provide a throwing station of approximately 30' in length. The objective is to throw two different sized footballs at targets mounted on the wall. Some type of score needs to be derived for these efforts. Each student should first get five chances, (using an overhand throwing motion in both cases) first throwing a regulation size football (H.S. varsity type) then using a junior size football in the second throwing attempt.

c. Accommodating development (strength). This station would be conducted similarly to the accommodating growth (hands) station above: substitute a basketball and a medicine ball as the equipment. Each student should get two puts (shotput-style tosses) using first the basketball, then two chances using a medicine ball. Scores are kept on the basis of distance generated in the tosses.

d. Accommodating development (balance). Again, this station would be conducted similarly to those above. This time substitute two (more if available) sets of stilts. Determine how long each student can balance (movement while balancing is permitted). First on a pair of stilts with the foot support blocks 6" off the floor, second, with a pair of stilts with the foot support blocks two feet off the floor.

5. At the close of the lesson, draw the students together and discuss their written comments based on their observations at each station. After discussing the above, and time permitting, the following two questions could also be raised in general discussion:

1. Have there been any situations in previous lessons in physical education class where the environment could have been changed to better accommodate the growth and development characteristics of any individuals in the class?

2. Do you see application for what you learned today in any out-of-school activities?

Materials Needed:

- medicine balls, basketballs, tennis balls, and footballs (regulation size *and* junior or intermediate size)
- floor hockey game equipment
- stilts (two sizes)
- tape
- "Analyzing the Learning Environment" forms and pencils

Evaluation:

A perusal of the comments made on "Analyzing the Learning Environment," plus the content of the discussion that takes place during class, should provide sufficient information to establish the degree to which the lesson's objective was met.

Related Concepts:

- Growth in height and weight alters the mechanical nature of physical performance (V6, P17)
- Motor development reflects changes in a person and changes in how they interact with their environment (V6, P2)
- Sex differences are found in growth rates (V6, P10)
- Height is basically determined by genetic factors (V6, P10)
- Muscle growth parallels general body growth (V6, P15)
- Growth generally improves physical ability (V6, P17)
- Performance quality is influenced by maturity and experience (V6, P17)

An environment that accommodates the growth and development characteristics of students optimizes the potential for learning motor skills.

ANALYZING THE LEARNING ENVIRONMENT

Name _____ Grade _____

Please read this before you start today's activities: The learning environment can have a positive or negative effect on student learning. While growth and development patterns are similar for all students, individual growth rates vary. Your task in this lesson is to identify how you and/or your peers were affected by growth and developmental characteristics while performing the activities at each station.

Station #1—Accommodating the growth characteristic: height

A-1 Did you execute skill better, the same, or worse when you were required to grip the hockey stick handle below the tape?
(Explain your answer in some detail).

A-2 What observations did you make concerning *your peers* with regard to the question in A-1?

A-3 As a result of your experience at Station #1, what can you say about the need to accommodate the learning environment of a class in relation to the growth characteristic of height?

Station #2—Accommodating the growth characteristic: size of hands.

Score, smaller ball _____ larger ball _____.

B-1 Did you execute skills better, the same, or worse when you used the regulation size football? Why?

B-2 What observations did you make concerning *your peers* with regard to question B-1?

B-3 As a result of your experience at Station #2, what can you say about the need to accommodate the learning environment of a class in relation to the growth characteristic of hand size?

Station #3—Accommodating the developmental characteristic: strength.

Score, lighter ball _____ heavier ball _____.

C-1 Were you able to execute the skill better, the same, or worse when you used the medicine ball? Why?

continued

Analyzing the Learning Environment continued

C-2 What observations did you make concerning *your peers* with regard to question C-1 above?

C-3 As a result of your experiences at Station #3, what can you say about the need to accommodate the learning environment of a class in relation to the developmental characteristic of strength?

Station #4—Accommodating the developmental characteristic: balance.

D-1 Did you execute skill better, the same, or worse when you used the stilts with the highest foot rests? Why?

D-2 What observations did you make concerning *your peers* with regard to question D-1 above?

D-3 As a result of your experience at Station #4, what can you say about the need to accommodate the learning environment of a class in relation to the developmental characteristic of balance?

Topic: Growth Rates

Individual growth rates vary (V6, P8)

Research indicates that while growth patterns are very constant, rates of growth vary. It is important for both children and teachers to understand this concept as it is critical to the teaching-learning situation. When students are behind or ahead of their chronological peers, two potentially incorrect assumptions may be made by either the teacher, student, or both. Inasmuch as performance is influenced by maturity, the chronological peers who have slower growth rates than their peers may feel inferior in skill development. The students must understand the role maturity plays in skill development and how growth occurs. Similarly, the students who appear to be more skilled than their peers must realize the difference may be temporary.

As a result of the learning experiences students should be able to record and graph their own growth patterns as determined by height and weight measures.

Learning Experiences:

Understanding growth rates

This can be used as a classroom experience when gymnasium facilities are not available.
1. Discuss the points covered in the discussion and indicate the objective of the learning experience.
2. Provide each student with a "Height and Weight Chart".
3. Collect data using at least four stations. Two stations utilize simple bathroom scales which the children use to get weight measurements. Two stations use prearranged strips of masking tape or measuring tapes placed on the walls. Each strip accurately marks off 6′ in quarter inch marks. Two L-shaped pieces of wood can be nailed together and used to establish specific heights.
4. After the information is collected and recorded, students can begin graphing or continue established graphs of their height and weight growth rates.
5. The students and teacher can then discuss the information by asking questions such as the following:
   a. Do the data indicate the same growth rates between September and January as it does between January and May? Have students speculate as to why the differences (if any) may have occurred.
   b. Do this year's growth rates parallel last years? (Data should be acquired at least twice a year.)
   c. Does anyone show a weight loss between September-January or January-May? If yes, to what is the loss attributed? (There is opportunity here for the teacher to

possibly detect a concern which should be brought to the attention of school medical personnel, i.e., significant weight losses in children do not represent typical growth patterns.)

There are many other questions that the teacher could ask to stimulate discussion and/or to convey the concept.

6. The data should be sent home to the parents via the students (possibly with the report cards). The form should be signed by the parents and returned to the physical educator. This lesson has many benefits beyond developing a concept, not the least of which is the public relations effect. Parents generally are intrigued by the data collected on their children and appreciate the data collecting efforts of the teacher.

7. This lesson could be activated at any time there is ample data on each student's personal growth card. The collecting of the data (heights and weights) could comprise one station on a day when multiple station activities are being offered.

Materials Needed:

- scales
- measuring tapes and measuring guides
- "Height and Weight Chart"
- "Cumulative Height and Weight Chart"

Evaluation:

By show of hands, have the children indicate the time frame of their greatest weight gain, then their greatest height gain. Ask each class member to indicate in one or two paragraphs why everyone in the class did not show maximum gains in the same time frame. Their written answers should provide sufficient evaluative information regarding their understanding of relevant concepts.

Related Concepts:

- Growth occurs in definite patterns (V6, P8)
- Sex differences are found in growth rates (V6, P10)
- Performance quality is influenced by maturity and experience (V6, P17)

_____ School

Height and Weight Chart

Name _____ _____

parents please
initial here

1st Grade   Height ____   Height ____   Height ____   Jan. _____
  September Weight ____   January Weight ____   May Weight ____   May _____

2nd Grade   Height ____   Height ____   Height ____   Jan. _____
  September Weight ____   January Weight ____   May Weight ____   May _____

3rd Grade   Height ____   Height ____   Height ____   Jan. _____
  September Weight ____   January Weight ____   May Weight ____   May _____

4th Grade   Height ____   Height ____   Height ____   Jan. _____
  September Weight ____   January Weight ____   May Weight ____   May _____

5th Grade   Height ____   Height ____   Height ____   Jan. _____
  September Weight ____   January Weight ____   May Weight ____   May _____

6th Grade   Height ____   Height ____   Height ____   Jan. _____
  September Weight ____   January Weight ____   May Weight ____   May _____

7th Grade   Height ____   Height ____   Height ____   Jan. _____
  September Weight ____   January Weight ____   May Weight ____   May _____

8th Grade   Height ____   Height ____   Height ,____   Jan. _____
  September Weight ____   January Weight ____   May Weight ____   May _____

Parents: Please note your child's height and weight gains over the academic year. Also, please initial in the
    space provided and have your child return the card to me. Thank you!

CUMULATIVE HEIGHT AND WEIGHT CHART

Name _____   School _____

HEIGHT

6.0	
10	
8	
6	
4	
2	
5.0	
10	
8	
6	
4	
2	
4.0	
10	
8	
6	
4	
2	
3.0	

S J M   S J M   S J M   S J M   S J M   S J M
yr ____ yr ____ yr ____ yr ____ yr ____ yr ____

CUMULATIVE HEIGHT AND WEIGHT CHART

Name _____ School _____

WEIGHT

180																		
175																		
170																		
165																		
160																		
155																		
150																		
145																		
140																		
135																		
130																		
125																		
120																		
115																		
110																		
105																		
100																		
95																		
90																		
85																		
80																		
75																		
70																		
65																		
60																		

S J M   S J M   S J M   S J M   S J M   S J M

yr _____ yr _____ yr _____ yr _____ yr _____ yr _____

Topic: Methods In Skill Development

Practice length and organization should vary according to the difficulty and type of skill and age, skill and intelligence of the learner (V3, P38)

The rate at which a student can learn a new skill is dependent on numerous variables, among which maturity and experience are very important. Skills are sometimes best learned in parts, by practicing one aspect of a total skill at a time. Other skills are best learned as a whole, where the entire skill is practiced at one time.

In the case of sequential skills where body actions follow in a particular order, for example, a gymnastics routine or a folk dance where each part is distinct and can stand alone, it is best to use the part method. In a skill such as a lay-up where parts of the skill are not very distinct, it is best to teach/learn the skill as a whole. For sports comprised of many independent skills (volleyball, tennis, etc.) it is best to use the whole-part-whole method. Mini-game or controlled game (lead-up) situations are effective in learning these types of activities.

As a result of the learning experience the student should:

1. Be able to indicate if specified skills (see 6A-D) should be taught/learned via the part or whole approach.
2. Experience the frustration of attempting to learn a rhythmic routine using an incorrect method.
3. Experience the potential satisfaction, pleasure, and joy of being a contributing member of a coordinated unit.

Learning Experiences:

Applying whole and part learning methods

Note: This activity is only appropriate if all class members have previously accomplished basic level dribbling skills.

1. Discuss the concepts from the discussion section and indicate the objectives of the learning experience (see 1–3 above).
2. Indicate that the first experience will involve using an incorrect method of learning in relation to the activity to be learned.
3. Demonstrate the complete basketball skill routine to the music of Alley Cat then ask the students to perform the routine. Direct attention to personal frustration and the frustration of the class as the group efforts "break down."
4. Demonstrate, in parts, the particular skills that accompany the different musical phrases. Review each part in sequence gradually putting the entire routine together (part method).

Note: The following is just an example. Creative teachers will most likely want to create their own routines to other music using different skills.

The Alley Cat basketball skills routine:

There are two basic phrases in the music and they are referred to as A and B. These phrases are repeated throughout the song. Each phrase has a total of 32 beats (8 4/4 measures).

Following a three note introduction, complete this sequence each time the A phrase is heard.

A Phrase

1st (8) Dribble 7 times (to the beat) with the right hand then catch the ball with both hands on the 8th beat.

2nd (8) Dribble 7 times with left hand—catch ball on the 8th beat.

3rd (8) Alternate 7 times right and left hands—catch ball on 8th beat.

4th (8) Make 4 quarter-turn pivots (including a fake pass with each pivot completing 360° in 8 counts.

The A phrase will then be repeated for another 32 counts as in the sequence of movements indicated directly above.

B Phrase—(First time played—32 counts)

1st (8) Throw jump ball on 5th beat and rebound on 6th through 8th beats. Participants throw up jump ball as if they were referees. After the ball is tossed each person rebounds toss as a player would rebound.

2nd (8) Throw jump ball on 5th beat and rebound on 6th through 8th beats. Participants throw up jump ball as if they were referees. After the ball is tossed each person rebounds toss as a player would rebound.

3rd (8) Throw jump ball on 5th beat and rebound on 6th through 8th beats. Participants throw up jump ball as if they were referees. After the ball is tossed each person rebounds toss as a player would rebound.

4th (8) Make a 360° turn dribbling the ball 7 times using dominant hand and catch the ball on the 8th beat and be ready to begin the A phrase again.

B Phrase (The second time the B phrase will be played *follows* 3 repetitions of the A phrase.)

1st (8) Make a one handed pass with your dominant hand to a person nearby. Take the first five notes to find someone to pass to on the 6th note. The receiver should receive the ball on the 8th note.

2nd (8) Make a one handed pass with the dominant hand to a person nearby. Take the first five notes to find someone to pass to on the 6th note.

3rd (8) Make a one handed pass with the dominant hand to a person nearby. Take the first five notes to find someone to pass to on the 6th note.

4th (8) Make a 360° turn dribbling with non-dominant hand using seven dribbles. The A phrase is repeated for 32 beats.

C Phrase (the last 16 counts of the song following the last A phrase) are done as follows:

1st (8) Make 360° turn dribbling 7 times with your dominant hand.

2nd (8) Make 360° turn dribbling 7 times with your non-dominant hand.

Throw the ball up in the air—catch it and sit down.

Instruct the students to listen carefully as to how the A phrase sounds because they should always follow the same content sequence whenever they hear that phrase. The whole song follows this sequence:

A (32 counts) A (repeated 32 counts) B (32 counts) A (repeated 32 counts). All of the above is then repeated a 2nd time.

A (32 counts) A (repeated 32 counts) B (32 counts) A (repeated 32 counts) then C which consists of a final tag of 16 counts.

5. **Variations:**
The B phrase can be used to introduce other basketball skills such as:
   a. Shooting—Make targets on walls to serve as imaginary baskets if baskets are not available.
   b. Make the pass to a partner (B phrase) more difficult by passing to three different people on each of the 3 passes. Allow only non-verbal behavior (eye-contact) to be used to identify the pass receivers.
   c. Once the entire routine is well known, allow participants to knock balls away from others during the playing of the ''A'' phrase. However, each participant must keep the beat to the music with the ball while attempting to knock a ball away from another person.
   d. Having the students indicate whether each of the following should be taught using whole or part method. Be sure they give specific reasons for their answers (The teacher should explain the whole-part-whole method when item C below is discussed:

Activity:	Answers:
A. Dribbling	(whole, because it is one integrated skill)
B. Gymnastic routine	(part because various tricks can stand alone)
C. Breast stroke	(whole, part, whole, but whole should be used as soon as appropriate. The leg motion and the arm motions can stand alone)
D. Overhand throw	(whole, because follow through will result if other aspects of the throw are performed correctly.)

   E. Question: what method was used in the lesson just taught? Answer: Whole, part, whole, but, initially the parts were too concentrated to allow for effective learning.

Materials Needed:

• record player and records (Alley Cat or other similar records)
• any type of ball, one per student

Evaluation:

The questions and answer aspects of #5 above should serve as an adequate source for evaluation.

Related Concepts:

- A number of factors affect choice of whole or part practice (V3, P36)
- Start by practicing the whole skill and modify practice as needed (V3, P37)

Skills are sometimes best learned in parts, by practicing one aspect of the total skill at a time.

Topic: Mental Practice

Mental practice can improve performance (V3, P35)
Combining mental and physical practice can result in maximum improvement (V3 P35)

Students should learn that performance can be improved through mental practice. Mental practice works well with closed skills but not as well as physical practice. A combination of mental and physical practice seems to be better than physical practice alone. Mental practice in combination with equal amounts of physical practice seems to work with open skills in a few studies where it has been tested.

As a result of this learning experience the student should demonstrate the effects of mental practice in the closed skill of putting.

Learning Experiences:

Experiencing Mental Practice

1. Discuss the concepts from the discussion section and indicate the objective of the learning experience.
2. Divide the students into pairs. Provide each pair with two improvised golf clubs or plastic floor hockey sticks, two tennis size yarn balls (use tennis balls if activity is conducted outside) one hula hoop and one numbered pylon or plastic bowling pin.
3. Allow the students to practice the putting stroke by progressively moving back 5' whenever four putts in a row go into the hula hoop. (This learning experience presumes previous instructional experiences in this skill.)
4. After 5–10 minutes of physical practice conduct a mental practice. Have students close their eyes and repeat what the teacher says, at the same time "feeling" that they are doing what the teacher is saying (see "Mental Practice-Putting.") The teacher will verbalize the series of thoughts as the students repeat what the teacher says. After 5 repetitions by the teacher students should then be asked to repeat quietly the series of thoughts to themselves 10 more times.
5. After finishing the mental practice the students can either have 5 more minutes of regular putting practice or begin playing on a putt-putt course designed by the teacher.

Materials Needed:

- improvised golf clubs or plastic floor hockey sticks
- yarnballs or tennis balls
- hula hoops
- pylons or plastic bowling pins
- "Mental Practice—Putting" handouts

Evaluation:

Discuss with the students the validity of mental practice and ask if anyone seemed to benefit from the mental practice. Ask for detailed explanations.

Related Concepts:

- How the learner practices is the key to improving performance (V3, P29)
- Some skills require manipulation of objects (V3, P23)
- Closed skill practice requires an unvarying environment (V3, P34)

Mental Practice—Putting

The teacher states the following list slowly 5 times as students memorize the words and imagine performing the skills as the list is read. Students then individually administer the list to themselves 10 times. (The list may be reproduced in the form of handouts or placed in large print on a chalkboard so that it may be referred to by students if forgotten.)

Students close eyes and imagine that they are doing the following:

- Head over ball—relax hands, shoulders, and arms

- Slow straight backswing

- Feel a smooth ending in backswing

- Smooth forward swing line *through* the ball

- Head still—listen for the ball to hit the target

Topic: Force Production

Force is needed to produce or change motion (V2, P1)
As muscles contract they create internal forces (V2, P2)
Gravity, friction, and fluid resistance are examples of external force (V2, P2)

It is important that the learner of movement skills understand how to generate force. The application of appropriate force is an integral element of any motor skill. There are two fundamental sources of force production: internal and external force. Muscles create internal force by contracting. Gravity, friction, and fluid resistance are examples of external forces. External forces must frequently be overcome or sometimes used advantageously by the mover in order to facilitate a skillful movement.

Important sub-concepts for development in this lesson are momentum, center of gravity, and the affect of body position in the stabilization of opposing forces.

As a result of these learning experiences the student should: be able to verbalize specific practical examples of inertia and friction and successfully complete a work page on the material learned with application to motor skill development.

Learning Experience:

Understanding external and internal force application as it relates to movement skills

1. Discuss the concepts from the discussion section and indicate the objective of the learning experience. Specify to the learners that they are to look for the effects of friction and inertia in these lessons.
2. Indicate that the activities are not only designed to help students understand force, but to help in the development of strength and balance.
3. Divide the students into groups of three's. One person will sit down on a rug (approx. 2' × 4'), burlap, potato, or seed bag, or on three carpet squares (one under the buttocks and one under each foot). The two other members of the group will become "pullers", that is, the suppliers of muscle power (internal force). Each puller will hold a rope and the "rider" will hold one end of each of those ropes. The pullers will then pull the rider in a straight line to a prescribed point. A change in riders and pullers should then be made as the same activity is repeated in opposite directions two more times, thus giving each member of the threesome a chance to be the rider. Repeat the series an appropriate number of times until a rest period is needed. Competition

against time or other groups may be used for motivation purposes if desired, but keep the lesson focused on force production. Use verbal clues to direct student attention to some of the desired learning outcomes indicated on the "Worksheet on Force Production." This activity can be used as a warm-up for other class activities or additional activities using the carpets can be utilized when the students become skilled in the safe use of the materials. Additional activities include:

a. "Chariot races" or "Auto races" on the carpets racing around an oval course in the gym.
b. "Water skiing," the rider kneels or stands on two carpets while being pulled by two teammates.
c. "Skating relays" on the carpets.

Note: Activities a and b can be dangerous if the students are not well skilled in dynamic balance and if they don't understand the potential problems such as not giving the rider sufficient room to make turns, etc.

4. Have students respond to questions such as those that follow and/or use the "Worksheet on Force Production."

a. What part of the pull is most difficult? (Answer: the start—overcoming inertia.) Ask why this is the most difficult.
b. The moment the pullers stopped pulling the person on the carpet, the carpet did not come to a stop. What caused the rider to stop? (Answer: friction and loss of power.) How does the word momentum relate to the question asked above? (Answer: the amount of space covered after the pulling force was stopped was due to momentum.)
c. Name a motor skill activity in which the players have to estimate the effect of friction in order to know how much force to apply. (Answer: shuffleboard—many other answers would also be appropriate.)

Materials Needed:

- a sufficient number of any one or combination of these three: Carpet squares (12" × 12"), burlap potato sacks, or rugs (2' × 4')
- a sufficient number of 6' ropes—two per each group of three students
- "Worksheet on Force Production"

Evaluation:

Have students complete the "Worksheet on Force Production" and/or conduct a discussion using its content.

Related Concepts:

- External forces will produce or alter movement (V2, P20)
- Kinetic friction develops when an object moves across another (V2, P20)
- Sliding friction is a gripping force (V2, P24)
- Size, shape, surface, and speed of movement affect the amount of resistance (V2, P22)

Name _____   Class _____

Lesson: Understanding external and internal force application as it relates to movement skills

Worksheet on
Force Production

1. A person *sliding* into second base is an example of which external force demonstrated in class? (Answer: Friction)

2. What determines how far away from second base a runner should begin a slide? (Answer: Velocity (speed) and friction).

3. The beginning forward movement of a person being pulled on a carpet is an example of overcoming _____. (Answer: Inertia)

4. When the pullers let go of the ropes while pulling someone on a carpet, the external force that stopped the person on the carpets is called _____. (Answer: Friction)

5. What does a sprinter do just prior to the sound of the starting gun in order to help overcome inertia? (Answer: Center of gravity is lifted and positioned forward in the direction of the finish line. Legs are in flexed position ready to extend.)

6. How should the rider exert internal force in order to better stabilize position? (Answer: The rider exerts internal force by leaning back away from the force of the pullers.)

7. As the "pullers" are about to begin pulling, what should they do in relation to the position of their centers of gravity? (Answer: Lower their centers of gravity and extend them forward in order to establish better stability and to be in a better position to initiate internal force to overcome inertia.)

Topic: Projecting Force: Passing and Shooting a Basketball

A projectile moves under the influence of the projecting force, gravity, and air resistance (V2, P48)

Many specific skills are included under the term *throwing* (a way to project force). The three basic throwing patterns are underhand, overhand, and sidearm. There are a few special types of throws such as throwing a frisbee, or shooting a basketball. However, most throws fit into one of the three patterns listed above.

The purpose of the throw dictates the type of throw to be used. The student in physical education should not only know how to throw, but also which throwing pattern to use in specific situations. To know which throw to use and having a knowledge of how throwing force is achieved are both essential for successful execution.

There are four basic parts involved in a throw and the correct application of each part is critical to achieving a satisfactory result. The four elements involved in projecting a throwing force are:

a. Length of backswing.
b. Use of appropriate number of body segments to generate the force necessary.
c. Adding body parts to the throw sequentially (timing).
d. Speed of movement in the body parts used.

Throwing involves the effective use of a through d above. Additionally, body strength, particularly in the arms, shoulders, and torso, are important attributes for a thrower. The teacher should discuss appropriate exercises to develop strength in these areas.

The planned lesson is experimental (problem solving) in that the learners are asked to find the most effective throwing style for the task indicated and for their current ability level.

As a result of this learning experience the student should be able to make knowledgeable (insightful) decisions concerning the efficient and effective projection of a ball in various situations.

Learning Experiences:

Experimentation in projecting a ball

1. Discuss the concepts from the discussion section and indicate the objective of the learning experiences.
2. Divide the class into groups to equalize the number of participants at each station. Have as many stations as facilities will permit. Identify each station with a large number so that initial placement at a station and station rotation will be facilitated.
3. Supply each student with a copy of the "Basketball—Shooting and Passing" form. Assign students to each station and allow the experimentation to begin. Allow the amount of time necessary to complete the necessary experimentation at each station, then have the students rotate to the next station (students at the highest numbered station would rotate to station #1). Provide time to record notes related to their experimentation. Initially, the instructor should indicate to the students that experimentation and/or recording written notes should continue until a station rotation is called for by the instructor.
4. Conclude the activities when the experimentation has been completed or when a sufficient time for the closing of the lesson requires stopping.
5. At the conclusion of the experimentation, gather the students together to discuss their results as they apply to efficient and effective force production. Some items for additional discussion may include:

Maximum distance shot, set shot:	Use of lower body parts (legs)? Adding body parts sequentially (timing)?
Most forceful pass:	Length of backswing? Telegraphing aspect of long backswing? Catchability—certain passes are not good at close range if they are too difficult to catch.
Most accurate pass:	Middle level is the most utilized level in skill practice. Short distance needed to generate necessary power. It's not like a baseball pass.
Maximum distance shot, one hand jump shot:	Body height production? Use of ankles, knees and hips? Center of gravity? Location of? Limitation of body parts in shooting force production due to lack of base of support.
Most effective pass against defender:	Low level (bounce pass) is difficult to intercept for at least two reasons: ● The time it takes for defender to move from middle to low level. ● Less practice in movement at low level makes interception more difficult.
Most effective rebound (outlet) pass:	Airborn body turn. Security of two hands. Short preparatory motion (backswing). Body segment of importance—wrist snap.

Materials Needed:

- one basketball, or other similar ball, for two people
- two basketball standards (More stations and more tasks could be created if more standards are available, especially if class size exceeds twenty-four)
- "Basketball—Shooting and Passing" forms and pencils

Evaluation:

A review and discussion of the results of the experimentation during the closing phase of the lesson should serve as a sufficient evaluation about whether or not the lesson's objectives have been met.

References:

Portions of this learning experience were extracted from ideas and materials from Kathy Nelson, University of Wisconsin at LaCrosse.

Related Concepts:

- Speed of movement of body parts affects amount of force developed (V2, P55)
- Sequential movement of body parts generates force to be imparted to the object at release (V2, P54)
- Use maximum number of body segments to increase force (V2, P55)
- The summation of forces will increase force (V2, P55)
- A follow through facilitates projection at maximum velocity (V2, P49)
- Force will be reduced if firm contact is not maintained at the moment of contact or release (V2, P49)

Basketball—Shooting and Passing

Name _____ Date _____

Directions: Starting at the station indicated by the instructor, with a partner, experiment to find the answers to the following questions:

Station #_____ Find the maximum distance you can shoot a one handed set shot and hit the rim (or backboard) 4 out of 5 times. Answer in feet _____.

Station #_____ Find the most forceful pass you can throw (consider distance, speed, and effectiveness, i.e., was it reasonably catchable?)

Describe the pass:

Station #_____ What is the most accurate pass you can find to hit a 2 foot square on the wall from a distance of 10 feet, 4 out of 5 times?

Describe the pass:

Station #_____ Find the maximum distance you can shoot a one hand jump shot and hit the rim (or backboard) 4 out of 5 times. Answer in feet.

Station #_____ Find the most effective pass to throw to a teammate when both the passer and receiver are being closely defended.

Describe the pass:

Station #_____ Bounce the ball high off the wall and catch it while jumping in the air. Before landing, make the most efficient and effective pass to a partner *before* your feet touch the floor.

Describe the pass:

> # Topic: Application of Force
>
> ## The point at which the force is applied affects the action (V2, P26)
>
> When force is used to generate or alter the motion of an object the point of application is critical. Basically, two types of movement can be generated, linear or straight lined motion and rotary or curved lined motion. A physically educated person should know the point at which force must be applied to an object in order to bring about a desired result in the most efficient and effective manner.
>
> As a result of this learning experience the student should demonstrate an understanding of the concept by correctly responding to 80% or more of the questions on the "Application of Force Worksheet" and by skillfully demonstrating an ability to move an obstacle effectively in the learning experience activity.

Learning Experiences:

Application of force to an object to bring about a specific reaction

1. Discuss the concepts from the discussion section and indicate the objective of the learning experience.
2. Indicate that the "Battleball" activities are aerobic in nature and that occasionally the class may be asked to take a 6-second pulse count in order to determine the aerobic demands of the activity. (Adding a zero to whatever number each student gets provides an indication of heart rate per minute.)
3. Divide the students into four comparable teams based on throwing skills. Have each team, 4–10 students, line up between two traffic cones so that four 30'–40' sides of a square are formed. Explain the rules of the game: each person starts out with a ball (playground ball, foam football, soccer, or volleyball). In the middle of the square a 24" cage ball is placed. On the word "go" each student throws at the cage ball while staying behind the goal line being defended. The object of the game is to hit the cage ball and drive it across the opponent's goal line which is directly opposite their own line. Once the ball is thrown a student is free to retrieve any loose ball, but, the ball must be taken behind the goal line being defended before it can be thrown. When the cage ball crosses over any one of the four lines, the team directly opposite of the line the cage ball crossed scores a point. If at any time the cage ball touches a player, either intentionally or unintentionally, the team directly opposite of the player touched is awarded a point.

Ask the following questions each time a point is scored or 1–2 minutes elapses without a score:

1. At what point on the cage ball should a thrower attempt to hit? (See the "Application of Force Worksheet.") If the cage ball is struck in the top portion, a glancing hit

without full impact might result. A full impact hit in space 2 would be best because the ball is less stable nearer the top, and it would facilitate an overspin (top spin) on the ball thus bringing about a desirable rolling action. Always ask students to provide specific reasons for their responses.

2. To make the cage ball move in a linear (straight line) direction, at what position should the thrower attempt to strike the cageball? A central application of force is used to move an object in a straight line.

3. At what position should the cage ball be struck if the thrower wanted to have the cage ball spin (curve) to the left? Spin occurs when force is applied off-center, for example, to the right side of the ball causing a spinning action to the left.

4. Why should the ball not be hit in position 6? Hitting the ball in position 6 would cause a backspin, and this would be contrary to the desired effect.

5. Other variations and implications relevant to "Battleball:"
   a. Specific types of throws can be used (practiced) in the game, for example, throwing the ball using only the non-dominant hand, using the two-handed overhead throw (soccer throw-in), or using soccer type passing (using the feet only).
   b. This game can be very vigorous. The teacher may want to provide the students with "strategy planning sessions" thus providing productive rest periods. These sessions are helpful in allowing students to exercise leadership, strategy, and critical thinking.
   c. The same game can be played in a classroom using yarn balls and a large (heavy) mylar balloon.

Materials Needed:

- Four traffic cones (pylons)
- one 24" cage ball
- balls for each participant
- "Application of Force Worksheet" and pencils

Evaluation:

Have students complete "Application of Force Worksheets" and/or discuss this concept with the class using the worksheet content as the basis for discussion.

Note: If the teacher prefers not to work with paper and pencils, a transparency could be made of the worksheet and projected on the wall or screen. Students then could be asked to indicate the numbers for the correct responses and discussion could follow.

Related Concepts:

- Rolling friction opposes an object's motion as it rolls across a surface (V2, P24)
- Motion occurs when the forces acting on an object are greater in one direction than in another (V2, P26)
- Spin results when force is applied off center of the object (V2, P33)

APPLICATION OF FORCE WORKSHEET

Name _____ Grade _____

"Battle Ball Game"

Indicate the number on the ball (diagrammed below) which *best* answers the question. In responding to each question, assume the ball is directly facing you.

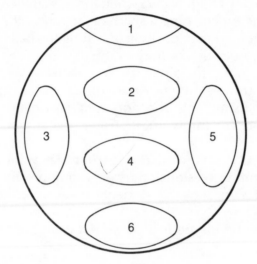

	Answers
1. To make the cage ball follow the most forceful straight forward line you should attempt to hit the cage ball in area:	_____ (2)
2. To make the cage ball take a spinning action partially forward and to the left, the thrown ball should strike area:	_____ (5)
3. To provide backspin to the cage ball it should be struck in area:	_____ (6)
4. To get the most top spin, the ball should be struck in area:	_____ (1)
5. If you were throwing from the x position on line C (see below) in the game "Battleball", and you wanted the cage ball to cross line A, you would attempt to hit the cage ball in area:	_____ (3)

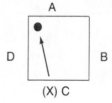

6. If you were pitching a baseball and wanted the ball to curve away from a left handed batter, on which numbers should your fingers apply the most pressure upon releasing the ball? (Assume that you pitch right-handed.)   _____ (3)

Topic: Spin Application

Spin results when force is applied off center of the object (V2, P33)

Many games require the application of spin to an object in order to optimize effectiveness. Baseball pitchers, for example, throw a variety of pitches. The action that each pitch takes is determined by a specific application of spin. Sometimes spin is applied to an object by another object: examples of this would be a bat in baseball, a golf club in the game of golf, a paddle in table tennis, or a racquet in racquetball.

Improperly applied, a spin can cause problems for a performer. An example of this would be slicing the ball in the game of golf.

There are four primary types of spin: backspin, top (over) spin, side spin right, clockwise, and sidespin left, counter-clockwise. To put spin on an object, force must be applied off center of the object.

As a result of this learning experience the student should demonstrate an ability to apply back, top (over), right, and left spins to a variety of objects.

Learning Experiences:

Spin With A Purpose

1. Discuss the concepts from the discussion section and indicate the objective of the learning experience.
2. Divide the class into four groups. Post written instructions at each station. Written instructions should indicate the experimentation expected at each of the stations. If desired, the instructor could provide a brief demonstration of the basic experimentation that should take place at each station in the introductory phase of the lesson.

Station #1—Use beach balls or vinyl balls (extremely light balls work best). Have the students practice applying pressure off-center in order to generate four spins: top (over), back, clockwise (right), and counter-clockwise (left). Work with a partner in making spinning bounce passes. Have students work individually against a wall when experimenting with back spin and top spin.

Station #2—Use hula hoops to experiment with back spin. Have students put back spin on a hula hoop so that it travels at least 15'–20' forward before the back spin takes effect. If skill is developed quickly, have students try to knock down targets (e.g., bowling pins) as the hula hoop completes the backspin phase of its travel.

Station #3—Use plastic bowling balls or playground balls. Have the student attempt to knock down a bowling pin(s) from an appropriate distance. Place an object about

4'–5' away, and directly between the student and the target. The student should attempt to have the ball curve (spin) around the object and knock down the pin.

Station #4—Use plastic whiffle balls and hockey sticks. Have the students apply clockwise spin (a slice) to a whiffle ball by striking it with a plastic hockey stick. When this is accomplished have the students attempt to apply counter-clockwise spins (hooks). Indicate that while conducting this experimentation, students should note the pathway the stick takes in order to bring about the slicing and hooking actions.

3. Some examples of questions that could be asked at the close of the lesson include:
A. What type of spin should be put on a shot at a basket? (Answer: back spin. Back spin brings the ball down at a more vertical angle as it rebounds off the backboard. Also, if the shot misses, the ball will stay closer to the basket for a rebound opportunity.)
B. What did you discover about the pathway the golf club took when a slice or a hook was applied?
C. What is the basic rule of force application to bring about spin? (Answer: force must be applied off center of the object.)
D. The instructor, while demonstrating the throwing action to be taken when curving a ball (the ball is not actually thrown) can ask the students which way the ball would spin if released.
E. What controls the timing of when spin will take effect? (Answer: the amount of linear velocity. The slower an object is moving in a horizontal direction, the sooner spin will be effected.)
F. Information and questions pertinent to the related concepts could also be discussed.

Materials Needed:

- beach balls or light vinyl balls
- plastic golf or hockey sticks
- bowling balls (plastic or cork) or playground balls
- hula hoops

Evaluation:

An objective observation and assessment of the students while they are participating at the stations and during the closing part of the session should enable the teacher to determine if the objectives were met.

Related Concepts:

- The faster the top spin the faster the rebound (V2, P36)
- An object that skids is not affected by its spin while skidding (V2, P36)
- Spin in the direction of flight will cause the rebound to be closer to the surface than if the spin is opposite to the direction of flight (V2, P37)

photo courtesy of Roy Nash

In baseball, the action each pitch takes is determined by a specific application of spin.

Topic: Jumping and Landing

Developing skills involves use of the laws of motion and stability (V6, P31)

Not too many years ago, players preparing to participate in a jump ball situation would be seen waiting in a deep crouch position for the ball to be tossed up by the basketball official. Typically, this type of preparation for a jump ball is no longer seen. Today you will most likely see players either standing in a very slight crouch or no crouch at all. The reason for the change is that research has demonstrated that muscular force for jumping is increased when muscles are stretched quickly.

The student in physical education should become knowledgeable about the fundamental principles involved in the acts of jumping and landing. The students should understand what they can do to enhance efficiency and effectiveness in the three phases of a jump: preparation, flight, and landing.

There are two basic categories of jumps: they are vertical (e.g. a jump ball in basketball) and horizontal (e.g. the long jump in track and field). However, horizontal jumps like the long jump actually require projection of forces in both horizontal and vertical directions.

Finally, the student should know that there are 5 jumping patterns, some of which are not used in sports but are used in some dance and game activities. Jumping patterns are: foot to foot (hop); two feet to two feet (jump); one foot to the other foot (leap); two feet to one foot; and one foot to two feet. The student should experience all of these patterns in physical education classes.

As a result of the learning experience the student should be able to demonstrate an understanding of the principles of projection and absorption in various jumping and landing activities.

Learning Experiences:

Jumping In Sports

1. Discuss the concepts from the discussion and indicate the objective of the learning experience.
2. Have each student work with a partner and participate in the following activities:
   a. Jump and reach—have one student stand sideways against a wall and stretch arm (on wall side) as high as possible. The partner should mark the point of the highest finger tip. The jumper will then have the height of each jump recorded by the partner. Jumps should be taken in this order:
      1. Two tries jumping using only the ankles.
      2. Two tries using ankles, and knees.

3. Two tries using ankles, knees and hips.

4. Two tries using all body parts in a fast flexion-extension sequence.

b. Standing long jump—basically the same sequence as above is followed except the use of the arms is added.

1. Two tries jumping using only the ankles.

2. Two tries using ankles and knees.

3. Two tries using ankles, knees, and hips.

4. Add the forward and upward use of the arms to the jump.

5. Use all body parts in a fast flexion-extension sequence.

6. Have each student take a turn standing on a bathroom scale. Have the students move their arms in very slow motion as they are used in the long jump. Then have the student use the arms very quickly. The students should note the varying affects the two motions have on the weight indicator.

(Note: Jumping away from a wall, with heels touching or almost touching the wall, is a good inhibitor of arm use until such time the use of the arms is encouraged.)

c. Landing—Each student should use the following progression for jumping—landing, while paying particular attention to the feeling of impact for each jump:

1. Jump off a low level obstacle (no higher than one foot) onto a mat without any bending at the ankles or knees when landing. Then, make the same jump flexing the knees considerably when landing. Note the difference in the sensation of impact.

2. Provide equipment of varying heights (2–4 feet) and stress practice in the utilization of the same body parts used in initiating a jump to be used in absorption of the force of landing.

d. Watch partner take two long jumps (horizontal) and two "jump ball" (vertical) jumps. Note the general location of the center of gravity in each jump, and the angle of take off in each jump. What was the difference in arm function between the two jumps?

e. Have each partner take 5 running steps forward, jump into the air and land in a circle two feet in diameter (circle made of string or very light rope), located no more than two feet in front of the take-off line. Have students add to the above 1/4, 1/2, 3/4 and full turns in the air before landing in the circle. The purpose of this activity is to get across the point that the fast forward (horizontal) movement must somehow be converted to vertical force. (Example: the purpose of the hurdle step in springboard diving is "to rock" the body back over the take-off foot, that is, get the exertion of force aspect of the jump over the base of support in order to provide for a more forceful take-off.)

f. Provide each pair with a ball and ask them to create some movements, involving both partners, which involve jumping and landing skills. For example: Partner A, while facing a wall, throws a ball at the wall at a height which will require a jump in the air to catch the ball. While still in the air the student makes a 180° turn and throws the ball to a partner who must receive the ball while suspended in the air as a result of an efficiently timed jump. Partners reverse roles and repeat the process.

g. Lesson closing—discuss the following:

1. Ask students for comments regarding personal effectiveness in mobilizing the

summation of forces (ankles, knees, hips, etc.).

2. Name the two basic forms of jumping (vertical and horizontal).
3. Name each jumping pattern and describe an application of the pattern in a movement activity.
4. Where is the center of gravity located in the preparation stage of a standing long jump? (Answer: ahead of the feet.) Why?
5. Ask what someone might do to increase jumping ability. (Possible answers: strengthen thigh and calf muscles; lose body fat to decrease the work necessary to lift the body; practice jumping.) Ask students if they can think of other ways.

Materials Needed:

- mats
- chalk
- measuring devices
- balls
- ropes

Evaluation:

The students' responses to in class discussion should provide the teacher with sufficient insight with regard to the students' understanding of the concept being presented.

References:

Portions of this lesson were extracted from materials prepared by Judy Pace and Phil Esten, University of Wisconsin at LaCrosse.

Related Concepts:

- To lessen the rebound, increase the distance over which force is to be absorbed (V2, P29)
- Trajectory is dependent upon the vertical and horizontal velocities imparted at the time of projection, angle and height of release, and the external forces occurring during flight (V2, P48)
- The angle of projection influences the time the object will be airborne (V2, P48)
- Force will be reduced if firm contact is not maintained at the moment of contact or release (V2, P49)

Topic: Absorption of Force

Increase distance and size of area to absorb force (preliminary concept)

Although projecting force often seems to be a more dramatic aspect in skill performance, absorption of force is extremely important and in the case of an excellent catch, such as a running catch in a baseball game, it can also be dramatic.

Absorption of force takes on an added dimension of importance when aspects of safety are associated with its proper application. When appropriate applications of force absorption are practiced, injury and accident statistics decline. Learning how to fall is really a lesson in force absorption. The moving object should be slowed by increasing the distance through which the object moves after contact, and/or increasing the size of the area which is absorbing the force of the object. These practices will keep the risk of injury and the chances of the object rebounding from the body at a minimum.

Absorption of force in a skillful performance is typically related to catching (as in baseball, football, and volleyball) and in object placement strategy (as in tennis, badminton, and racquetball).

As a result of this learning experience the student should:

1. Demonstrate an ability to catch an object using the correct application of absorption of force principles.
2. Demonstrate an ability to safely absorb body weight in a falling situation.

Learning Experiences:

Giving In To Pressure

1. Discuss the concept from the discussion section and indicate the objectives of the learning experience.
2. Working with a partner, have each student experience catching a ball thrown by a partner:
   a) First, with the arm back as if in preparation to swing a tennis racket. Attempt to catch the whiffle ball 5 out of 5 times. The catcher should stand sideways to the thrower and attempt all catches with the hand even with or to the thrower's side of the body.
   b) Attempt the same task with the exception that the catcher's hand starts out well to the thrower's side of the body and "absorbs" the force of the throw with a backward movement of the hand and arm (A sort of reverse tennis swing, similar to preparing to hit a forthcoming ball).

c) Reverse roles of partners and go through the same routine.

d) Upon completion, have the students sit down and discuss the results and implications with their partners.

3. Landing: the basic understanding with regard to the absorption of force as it applies to landing on the feet is that flexion helps to absorb (reduce) force. Have one partner throw a whiffle ball (jump ball style) into the air so that the other partner can rebound it. The partner who threw the ball should observe to see if the jumper properly absorbs the downward force of the body weight by flexing at the ankles, knees, and hips. Each performer should get five turns both as "rebounder" and "thrower-observer". The observer should focus on the rebounder performing a quick flexing action of the ankles, knees, and hips, followed by a quick extension of these same body parts as they jump to get the ball. The landing should involve flexion of these same body parts in an effort to absorb force.

4. Running: have each partner line up (sprint start position—center of gravity forward over base of support) so that 5–6 fast steps forward can be taken followed by 10 more steps in a continuing straight line as speed is gradually decelerated. Have each partner take three turns doing this individually then as partners, one behind the other (one about 6 feet behind the other) and starting off on the teacher's signal. The purpose of this drill is to make sure runners decelerate in a straight line so that collisions with following runners are avoided. Repeat drill with the other partner leading.

5. Falling: have each student find a safe (sufficient space) location on a mat. The teacher should then have everyone assume a front leaning rest position on the mats (high level push-up position). Ask students to slowly lower their bodies to the mat. Explain that this is the basic movement in the safe absorption of body weight from a fall. The lowering of the body weight is slowed by internal force (arm and shoulder muscles) and the size of the area (the entire body) is increased to safely absorb all of the body weight. Have the students, as they demonstrate *individual* capability to succeed, begin falls to the mat using the following sequence. (*CAUTION: Do not proceed to last step with all students in the class.*)

   1. Fall from a kneeling position.

   2. Fall from a squat position.

   3. Fall from a standing position.

   4. Fall from a standing position facing one-quarter turn away from mat. Make a quarter turn as the body falls to the mat.

   5. Facing directly opposite the mat, student begins backward fall but turns body a ½ turn to absorb force as described above.

   Variation: In conducting the falling sequence, numbers 1 and 2 above often receive enthusiastic participation when done "by the ripples," creating a wave effect.

6. At the close of the lesson, discuss some of the questions related to criterion referenced observations that took place during the class. Examples: in the push-up position should the hands be placed on the mat outside the width of the shoulders? Why? Should the fingers and thumbs of the hands be placed flat on the mat? Why?

Should the fingers of the hands be spread or close together? Why? What effect did the mats have in experience #5? What two safety precautions were practiced in experience #4? (Answer: 1. Completed deceleration moving straight ahead to avoid collision with the runners following. 2. Brought forces to a gradual rather than an abrupt stop to avoid injury to body parts.)

Materials Needed:

- mats
- whiffle balls

Evaluation:

Through observation of the students performing the activities, the teacher should be able to determine subjectively whether the lesson's objectives were achieved.

Related Concepts:

- To lessen the rebound, increase the distance over which force is to be absorbed (V2, P29)
- To lessen rebound, increase the size of the receiving area (V2, P29)

AN INVITATION
FROM AAHPERD/NASPE

The American Alliance for Health, Physical Education, Recreation, and Dance, NASPE, and the many *Basic Stuff* authors cordially invite *you* to become a participating author and to design or share current learning experiences with other professionals throughout the United States. Using the format guidelines on the following page, please complete your Learning Experience, indicate your name and professional affiliation, and mail it to:

Acquisitions Editor
Basic Stuff Project
AAHPERD
1900 Association Drive
Reston, VA 22091

As soon as we have an adequate number of Learning Experiences, we will publish them under a title such as *The Best of Basic Stuff*.

Topic:_____

Grade Level: ☐ K–3   ☐ 4–8   ☐ 9–12

Goal: ☐ Personal Fitness   ☐ Skillful Moving   ☐ Joy, Pleasure, & Satisfaction

Concept:_____

_____ volume _____ page _____

Discussion *(introduction to concept, definitions, relationships, purposes, outcomes, etc.):*_____

_____

_____

_____

Conceptual Focus *(What are the main points of this topic?):*

1. _____

_____

2. _____

_____

3. _____

_____

Learning Experiences *(includes tasks, classwork, labs, homework, etc.—small tables, charts, and worksheets included here):*

1. _____

_____

2. _____

_____

3. _____

_____

Materials Needed:

● _____

● _____

● _____

Evaluation:

1. _____

_____

2. _____

_____

References *(need only if very specific references used or suggested):*

_____

_____

Related Concepts:

● _____ volume _____ page _____

● _____ volume _____ page _____

● _____ volume _____ page _____

Attach additional full page lab experiences, worksheets, take-homes, transparencies, duplicating masters, and other materials

chapter five

Joy, Pleasure, and Satisfaction

The two preceding chapters dealt with personal fitness and skillful moving. There is another aspect of physical education that, while not being as demonstrably efficacious as fitness and skill development, is, in fact, a very important component of the total program. In today's terminology, we refer to the subject under consideration in this chapter as the affective domain. The affective domain concerns the feelings and emotions of people. The two *Basic Stuff* Series I books that apply most significantly to this domain are *Psycho-Social Aspects of Physical Education* and *Humanities in Physical Education*.

It should be understood, however, that both skill development and fitness are related directly to affective development. Students will develop a stronger appreciation for activities involving fitness and/or skill if they have experienced some degree of joy, pleasure, and/or satisfaction in performing those motor or fitness activities. There is little doubt that understanding the objectives of this chapter will be easier for readers who have had positive affective experiences in fitness and/or skill development than it will be for those who have not have experienced the joy, pleasure, and satisfaction of engaging in physical activity. One of the reasons that many physical educators emphasize that students should have *fun* in physical education is that they believe pleasant and/or rewarding experiences are more likely to be repeated than negative ones.

To know the joy of making a perfect striking motion on a baseball, softball, or golf ball can only be appreciated thoroughly by those who have experienced it themselves. To know the pleasure of victory and the sadness of defeat in a competitive activity, and how to cope with either situation, is an important learning experience that can help in the development of a value system that will be used throughout a person's life. The satisfying feeling one gets after completing a vigorous workout—even though it may not have been regarded as fun—is a result of perseverance and mental discipline that can be learned through physical education. If properly physically educated, the participant also will experience the personal wellness benefits of the workout and will take pleasure in the outcome (product) of the experience.

The examples provided above are only a few of the many aspects to be explored in the affective domain. Learning to move skillfully and developing high levels of personal fitness will be enhanced when learned in relation to the values placed on them. If the value is not positive, it is unlikely that either motor skill or personal fitness efforts will continue. This chapter is an effort to develop learning experiences which will predispose students toward healthy, positive, immediate, and life long affective attitudes toward physical activity.

Topic: Moving and Feeling Good

Knowing what feels good increases understanding of the movement experience (V5, P2)

There are as many different interests, likes, and dislikes in a physical education class as there are students. In order to optimize the chances for students to discover activities that make them feel good, a variety of movement opportunities must be available and encouraged.

Often, feeling good about an activity is directly related to the achievement that has been experienced in the participation of that activity. What "feels good" may change from time to time and from activity to activity. Students should be challenged to identify activities they like, and to determine specific reasons for their choices. This knowledge about themselves may enable them to make more insightful choices about future potential participation in activities. Students also should be encouraged to try new activities and to evaluate them in terms of feeling good.

Determining the information indicated above is also very important for teachers as it will help them to learn more about the students. The information obtained should be used to develop appropriate curricular opportunities. It will also enable teachers to make suggestions to students regarding opportunities that may be available in their favorite activities in afterschool community programs.

As a result of this experience the student should demonstrate insight into the specific reasons particular activities "feel good" to them.

Learning Experiences:

What is it I like about the games I play?

Note: This experience may be used by the physical education teacher as a rainy day activity, or, the physical education teacher could provide this theme to the English teacher to be used as an assignment. The English teacher should share the papers with the physical education teacher before returning them to the students.

1. Discuss the concepts from the discussion section and indicate the objective of the learning experience.
2. Develop a list of all the potential aspects of activity which could lead to feeling good. Have the students spend a portion of a class period responding, in writing, the *specific* aspects they enjoy most about their individual "feel good" activities. For example, is it competition, individual responsibility for achievement, or emphasis on skill that makes an activity attractive to them? Students should be required to be very specific about why they like an activity.

3. Spend the final portion of the class having students identify the key aspects of an activity that makes it a favorite, for example: number of participants (individual, dual, team); affiliation needs (see Related Concepts below); the amount of strategy involved (low, moderate, or high level strategy); the type of personal relationship (cooperative, competitive, cooperative/competitive in nature); and/or the motor skills used.

4. After the class, the teacher should tally the number of times different activities were mentioned so that the overall interest levels in various activities can be assessed. These data should have implications for curricular planning, for individualizing, and for personalizing the teacher's knowledge of students.

Materials Needed:

● writing materials

Evaluation:

The classroom discussion and the written papers of the students should provide sufficient information for the teacher to make a subjective evaluation concerning the students' understanding of the lesson's objective.

Related Concepts:

● Participation in physical activity can be an important way of meeting affiliation needs (V4, P38)
● Cooperation toward a common goal helps affiliation (V4, P40)
● What feels good differs among participants (V5, P1)

Topic: Feeling Good in Competitive and Cooperative Activities

What feels good differs among participants (V5, P1)

A definition of feeling good would best be identified by each participant. Some persons might relate feeling good to the process involved in an activity, that is, the actual doing aspect of an activity. Others might relate feeling good to the product aspect, the end result of participation in an activity. Some might feel good about one aspect (process or product) and not even like the feeling the other aspect provides. It is important that the learner becomes aware of what feels good and what doesn't feel good with regard to physical activity. An understanding of both feelings (good and bad) will help the student and the teacher to make decisions in the best interest of the learner. For example, a person may not particularly like jogging but if it is believed that jogging is good for enhancing the quality of life (good health), the physical satisfaction (product) derived from jogging may be sufficient to continue to motivate participation (process) in this activity. However, if the jogger was exposed to other means of bringing about similar good feelings regarding health, the possibility exists that both the process and product of another activity may be pleasurable. The point is, then, that students should be exposed to a wide variety of activities so that the opportunity for optimal selection can be facilitated. Optimal selection would be an activity in which both the process and the product was joyful, pleasurable, and/or satisfying to the participant. Stress that students can learn to feel good in an activity and that there are ranges of feeling good *or* bad.

As a result of this learning experience students should be able to identify specific reasons as to why they have good, neutral, or bad feelings regarding various types of physical activities.

Learning Experiences:

What types of activities feel good to me?

1. Discuss the concepts from the discussion section and indicate the objective of the learning experience.
2. Provide each participant with a copy of "What Types of Activities Feel Good to Me?" Students will select a partner with whom they will experience activities at four stations. As students finish various stations, they should make appropriate individual comments in response to questions on the form. Completing the stations can be accomplished in one or two class periods.
3. The four stations should represent each prescribed category.

Solo-Self Testing:

Students would be given the opportunity to do any one or combination of the

following activities on their own:
a. jump rope to music
b. jog a measured course
c. engage in a weight training or calisthenics routine or combination thereof
d. perform activities of an individual nature similar to those above

Partner-Cooperation:
Work toward maximizing a team score (with partner) in any combination of activities:
a. maximum number of two-handed chest passes in one-minute without a drop
b. juggle three balls with a partner. Record the number of catches made without a drop
c. continuous volley count (using hand rackets) off a wall alternating hits between partners
d. any one or combination of the above or any other activities which would constitute challenging partner activities of a *cooperative* nature would be appropriate

Indirect Competition Activities:
Either individual and/or dual type activities in which participants compete against established standards of performance
a. As a team (two people), attempt to make as many lay-up shots as possible in a one minute period. Participants must alternate shots, but a common total of baskets made constitutes the team score. Post names and best team score on the record sheet provided at the station before rotating to the next activity station.
b. Individual indirect competition (one person against the class). Same activity as above except that it is done as an individual not as partners.
c. Convert other activities done as partners into individual activities where each participant's score will be compared to all of the scores in the class.

Direct Competition:
Do any of the activities listed under the three preceding categories but make them direct competition type activities in which one partner will come out the winner and the other partner the loser in each activity in which they engage.

4. After giving each pair an opportunity to participate in the four types of experiences, allow the students time to make additional comments and to summarize their remarks on the forms provided.
5. Indicate the results of the *indirect competition* by announcing the five best partner related activity scores and the five best individual activity scores.
6. As the students verbally respond to a request of the teacher to comment on the positive/negative aspects related to each category of activity, the teacher should summarize the comments on a chalkboard. When this is completed a thorough discussion should take place. Some ideas for discussion could include the following:
a. Rank order the four types of activities. Which category of activity did you like best? Why? (Require specificity in the response.) Which did you like least? Why? (Require specificity.)
b. Ask students if their feelings about an activity category were influenced by the results (product) of that type of activity that is, how students and/or their partners did in relation to the rest of the class. Why? (Require specific responses.)

Materials Needed:

- chalkboard and chalk
- equipment needed for this learning experience
- "What Types of Activities Feel Good To Me?" and pencils

Evaluation:

The discussion phase of this lesson and the evaluation of the worksheet "What Types of Activities Feel Good To Me" should provide the teacher with sufficient information regarding the students' learning and understandings.

Related Concepts:

- Knowing what feels good increases understanding of the movement experience (V5, P2)
- Feeling good means achievement (V5, P2)
- Feeling good means good health (V5, P2)
- What "feels good" changes from time to time and from activity to activity (V5, P3)

What Types Of Activities Feel Good To Me

Name _____ Date _____
Class _____

In today's lesson you will experience activity at four stations. Each station is different in the type of activity provided. As you experience each type of activity you should jot down your feelings concerning why you liked or didn't like a particular type of activity.

Solo—Self Testing—Individual Type Activities:

Like because:

Dislike because:

Partner/Cooperation Type Activities:

Like because:

Dislike because:

Indirect Competition Type Activities:

Like because:

Dislike because:

Direct Competition (Head to Head, Winner—Loser):

Like because:

Dislike because:

Topic: Goal Setting

Goals need to be realistic (V6, P56)

Setting goals for physical activity involvement helps us make changes. Goals should be set very carefully. They need to be: 1) realistic, 2) attainable, 3) relevant, 4) observable, and 5) measurable. Goals are more easily attained if they involve activities we like, or are activities in which we are motivated to participate.

It is senseless to set a goal we know we cannot accomplish. Perhaps the goal is too big, will take too long to achieve, or it is something that really is not too important to us.

As a result of this learning experience, the students will:

1. Identify one goal they would like to accomplish.
2. Be able to determine steps to take to reach the goal and obstacles that may arise to slow progress toward goal attainment.

Learning Experiences:

Setting Goals

1. Discuss the concepts regarding goal setting from the discussion section. Students can share ideas about previous experiences with setting goals.
2. Distribute "Setting Goals" handout.

Materials Needed:

- "Setting Goals" handout
- pencils
- self-testing equipment (e.g. sit and reach box, mats or sit ups, etc.)

Evaluation:

Both the student and teacher should share in evaluating this experience. Initially, the teacher needs to provide guidance regarding realistic goal setting, including reasonable timelines within the program constraints. Goals may be set for one grading period and evaluated summatively or formatively. Setting subgoals may help with formative evaluation.

Related Concepts:

- Satisfaction results from attaining goals (V6, P57)
- Personal goal setting fosters self and other acceptance (V6, P54)
- Achieving is more than winning (V5, P16)

SETTING GOALS

Name: _____ Class: _____

Date: _____

1. State one physical activity goal you wish to reach. By when?

2. List the people who might help you reach your goal:

3. Do you think you can reach your goal? Why?

4. List some of the possible problems that may keep you from accomplishing your goal.
   PROBLEMS:

   What can you do to help avoid these problems?
   STEPS TO AVOID PROBLEMS:

5. If you believe you can reach your goal and avoid the problems, what are the steps you plan to take.
   Step 1:

   2:

   3:

(If you do not believe you can reach this goal, decide on another one and complete this sheet.)

Topic: Increasing Self-Esteem

Self-esteem is an important aspect of self-concept (V4, P8)

Physical activity can help people feel good about themselves. It can also make them feel bad if the activity is too hard and success does not occur. Self-concept, however, can be positively affected by successful participation.

In order for success to occur, it is important to feel physically fit and capable of performing the skills required by the activity. It is, therefore, necessary to understand what we can and cannot do and who we are. We understand more about ourselves when we share ourselves with others, so it is important to talk to another person about it.

As a result of this learning experience, the students will:

1. Understand some of their strengths and weaknesses.
2. Be able to see that everyone is different and has unique needs.
3. Be capable of sharing *and* listening during self-disclosure activities.

Learning Experiences:

Ideas for Enhancing Self-Esteem

1. Discuss the information in the discussion section. Prepare the class for the lesson's intent. Explain the reasoning behind it without alluding to the follow-up activity.
2. Organize appropriate activities and designate certain individuals, preferably half the class (e.g., all with the color blue on, all with straight hair, etc.), to do one of the following things:
   a. use their non-dominant hand or foot in the activity
   b. travel sideways or backwards only
   c. not participate
   The idea is to create a discriminating situation. Following the activity, have students organize into partners (one designated as "different" during the activity and one that was not). Allow about five minutes for discussion (feelings, relationship to other experiences, etc.). Then discuss feelings and impressions as a whole group. Relate to specific incidences typical to physical education environments (e.g., poorly skilled, overweight, uncoordinated).
3. Allow students to choose their partner. Each pair shares information about self, family, hobbies, and favorite games. Each partner must then share with the class "the most positive thing about Joe is . . .". Variations: share how it feels to be different; share "what I would really like to be like."
4. Assigning permanent partner or small group affiliations helps facilitate feeling good. The teacher must be sensitive to the concept of self-esteem. Students will learn from

this modeling. If partners or groups stay together for a while, they can be encouraged to communicate, share ideas, and help each other. Each day a challenge can be presented to:
- help someone in class with a skill
- compliment someone for something
- speak to someone you have not spoken to in a while
- share a new idea with someone

A few minutes can be taken at the end of class for group members to discuss their progress toward the day's challenge.

Materials Needed:

- equipment needed for the activity.

Evaluation:

Evaluation should take place during the discussion. How did students communicate during the lessons? Were they good listeners and good sharers? When group activities were used, did group members communicate well? Achieve their goals?

Related Concepts:

- Self-disclosure can enhance self-concept (V4, P7)
- A positive and realistic self-concept helps us to feel good (V4, P2)

photo courtesy of Jim Kirby

Physical activity can help people feel good about themselves.

Topic: Partner Contracts

Affiliation is a very important human need (V4, P37)

The physical activity context provides an opportune setting to promote the development of interpersonal skills. As human beings, we have a need to be accepted by others. Interacting with others can help us understand ourselves by providing important evaluative information. We seek approval from others and enjoy giving feedback to them.

Feeling isolated and alone often retards our progress toward personal goals. Physical activity environments can help us feel a sense of affiliation. When we set specific goals for ourselves, it can be helpful to receive feedback from others. We need to receive information about strengths and weaknesses and similarities/differences. What others do and how they react to us affects our behavior.

As a result of this learning experience, the student will:

1. Assist a partner in achieving exercise goals.
2. Receive assistance from a partner in accomplishing personal goals.
3. Respect and show appreciation for a partner's help.

Learning Experiences:

Partner Exercise Contract

1. Discuss concepts from the discussion section regarding affiliation.
2. Distribute "My Exercise Contract" forms to all students. Have them individually complete these forms as homework.
3. Allow students to decide on an exercise partner. Students should explain their strengths and weaknesses relative to exercise. Further, they should explain their exercise goals.

Materials Needed:

- "My Exercise Contract"

Evaluation:

This contract provides an ideal form of evaluation, in that self-evaluation, peer evaluation, and teacher evaluation are all possible. A caution: do not penalize students if goals were a bit overzealous. Instead, help them modify their goals. Reward the process, not the product.

Related Concepts:

- Self-disclosure can enhance self-concept (V4, P7)
- Perceptions of similarity aid affiliation (V4, P40)
- Participation in physical activity can be an important way of meeting affiliation needs (V4, P38)

photo courtesy of Greg Merhar

When we set specific goals for ourselves, it can be helpful to receive feedback from others.

MY EXERCISE CONTRACT

NAME: _____

GOALS: (Daily) _____

             (Weekly) _____

_____

INCREASING MY PHYSICAL ACTIVITY:

1. _____ minutes per day on stretching for flexibility.

   ACTIVITIES: _____

2. _____ minutes per day on aerobic activities for improving cardiovascular endurance.

   ACTIVITIES: _____

3. _____ minutes per day on muscle strength activities.

   ACTIVITIES: _____

4. _____ minutes each weekend in activities that improve my fitness and skill.

   ACTIVITIES: _____

_____

REWARDS:

DAILY:

   My partner and I have agreed on the following daily awards. When I meet my daily goals, I will receive one of these rewards:

   a.

   b.

   c.

   d.

WEEKLY:

   My partner and I have agreed on the following weekly awards. When I meet my weekly goals, I will receive one of these rewards:

   a.

   b.

   c.

   d.

_____

I agree to work hard to accomplish my goals. My partner and I have discussed each goal and the support we will give one another.

_____   _____   _____
   Signature   Partner Signature   Date

Topic: Achievement, Winning, and Losing

Achievement is an individual phenomenon (V5, P21)

There is no denying the significant developmental role competition plays, but sometimes, and very frequently when young people are involved, competition is allowed to get out of control and the results are negative.

Students must learn that achievement and score are not inextricably linked. In fact, a team victory in an athletic event is actually the sum total of the combined *individual achievements* of members of the team. It is not infrequent that outstanding individual achievement is lost sight of because the team lost. For example: in a singles game such as tennis, when one loses by only a point or two to a competitor who has beaten him or her handily in past performances (assuming it was skill that made the score close), this experience should not be simply summed up with the words, "I lost", when in fact, high level personal achievement took place.

As a result of this lesson the learner should focus on achievement aspects of individual play irrespective of the game score.

Learning Experiences:

Win or lose, achievement is progress

1. Discuss the concepts from the discussion section and indicate the objective of the learning experience.
2. Indicate that the activity to be played is a good aerobic capacity conditioner. However, the activity will be used in this lesson to focus on individual achievement.
3. Divide the class into two equal teams (10–20 students per team) based on throwing and catching abilities. (Vest or pinnie identification is needed). The name of the game is *End Ball*. Divide each team into two even groups of forwards and guards. The guards protect bowling pins positioned in hula hoops. The forwards move the ball by passing to teammates. *The key rule is that players cannot move when they are in possession of a ball.* The ball must be passed to a teammate or, if close enough, thrown at a pin in an attempt to knock it down. Play starts with one or two players on each team in possession of a ball. Once play starts, each ball is open to the possession of any player who can get it. The game is over after an arbitrary 1–2 minute time period elapses or all the pins on one team are knocked down by the other team. When that does happen, the forwards and guards on a team trade places and another match begins. An original guard can become a forward if the pin being guarded is knocked down. A guard is not allowed to step into a hoop while protecting the pin. If guards knock down their own team's pin by unintentionally hitting the pin or the hoop with their bodies, that pin is considered down. If the opposing team members

knock an opponent's pin down in any way other than by hitting it with a thrown ball, the pin is re-set immediately. Pins may be attacked from any angle.

Variations: Play the game using feet only for passing and shooting at the pins. This variation is much more demanding on the cardiovascular system and games tend to last longer than when throwing is used.

Time-outs to rest can be used as strategy sessions for the next match.

4. The members of each team should decide which half of their players will play in the first series of 3 End Ball games and which will play in the second set of games.

5. While the first group of team #1 is playing the first group of team #2, each teammate sitting on the sidelines will keep an achievement chart on one specific teammate (see "Scouting/Achievement Report").

6. When the first set of games is over, teammate "A" will share with teammate "B" the achievement data collected. After a few minutes a new game will start and the achievement data collector and the player will exchange roles.

7. At the close of the lesson, the teacher will ask students to respond to the following.
   a. Raise your hand if your teammates had a better achievement record in some of the games that were lost than in the games their teams won. An indication of one or more raised hands gives credibility to the fact that individual achievement can surpass previous individual achievement even if a contest is lost.
   b. Does anyone's scoring data show a basically steady increase in achievement? To what might this phenomenon be attributed? (Some appropriate responses may be: more practice time in the activity, application of better strategy, etc.)

8. Keep the data collection sheets for use on days when the game is played again and relate to the effect of experience and maturity on achievement.

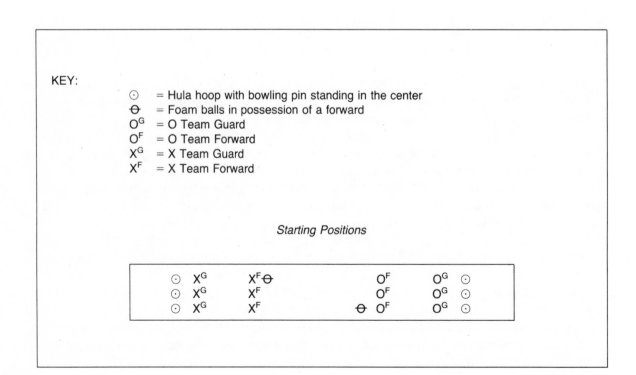

Materials Needed:

- foam balls (8½" size)
- hula hoops
- pinnies or identification vests
- copies of "Scouting/Achievement Report" and pencils
- plastic bowling pins

Evaluation:

The discussion that takes place following the game should enable the teacher to evaluate subjectively the accomplishment of the objectives.

Related Concepts:

- Spectators and athletes perceive different kinds of achievement in the same performance (V5, P19)
- Individual satisfaction is a motivating factor for participation (V5, P25)
- Achievement-related motives affect the ability to do better in activity (V4, P19)
- Attribution of cause affects performance in physical activity (V4, P28)

photo courtesy of Tom Trimble

During the "End Ball" game, students should focus on aspects of individual achievement, irrespective of the score.

SCOUTING/ACHIEVEMENT REPORT

Game: END BALL   Date _____

Player being observed _____

Observer (Scout) _____

Directions: The same scout keeps a tally during all three games. Under special comments note any special
              abilities the player exhibited such as: worked "give and go," faked opponent out of position,
              hustled for loose balls, defended well, etc. Circle *assists* when a pass results in a score by the
              player who received the pass.

FIRST SERIES OF THREE GAMES

	1st Game	2nd Game	3rd Game	Total
Successful Catches				
Successful Passes				
Shots at Target				

Special Comments:

Won_____ games of this Series, Lost_____ games

SECOND SERIES OF THREE GAMES

	1st Game	2nd Game	3rd Game	Total
Successful Catches				
Successful Passes				
Shots at Target				

Special Comments:

Won_____ games of this Series, Lost_____ games

Topic: The Element of Chance: The Unknown Lesson

Achievements contribute to self-identity (V5, P17)

Lessons in physical education class typically involve students participating simultaneously in the same activity. However, many times it is a better catalyst for learning and achievement if variety exists. We are constantly attempting to define our abilities. Self-understanding grows when we attempt new activities and gain a measurable sense of achievement. Therefore, variety, challenge, novelty, and a touch of mystery help us expand horizons.

As a result of this learning experience, the student will:

1. Be able to perform the activities indicated by the roll of the dice.
2. Be challenged optimally by the activities.

Learning Experiences:

The Role of the Dice

This activity can be modified for skill development or a combination of fitness and skill development.

Materials Needed:

- dice
- mats
- basketballs
- pace clock
- hand weights
- stretching chart
- jump ropes
- "Roll of the Dice Workout Chart"

Evaluation:

This activity could be recorded in a fitness activity log. Students should evaluate their own achievement while the teacher reviews log entries to determine the activity level of each student. A review and discussion of the effects of chance on participation choices during the closing phase of the lesson would be helpful.

Related Concepts:

- Individual satisfaction is a motivating factor for participation (V5, P25)

ROLL OF THE DICE WORKOUT CHART

1.	
Warm Up Workout Cool Down	*SNAKE EYE*—Roller's choice of activity. *Must:* 1) Stretching routine 2) Do 20 minutes of aerobic activity 3) Cool Down to heart rate <100.
2.	
Warm Up Workout Cool Down	*TERRIFIC TWOS*—1) 2 Minutes of Jogging 2) 2 Minutes of Stretches 3) 2—Ten minute aerobic routines 4) Walk around gym 2 times
3.	
Warm Up Workout Cool Down	*THREE'S COMPANY*—Partner Choice—Any two individuals rolling a three (3) must decide on partner activities. *GOAL:* After stretching, participate at least 20 minutes in the same aerobic activity, cool down.
4.	
Warm Up Workout Cool Down	*FOUR SQUARE*—Jog for 2 minutes and do stretching routine. Perform A four station circuit for 20 minutes (Teacher: design aerobic activities for circuit) Cool down.
5.	
Warm Up Workout Cool Down	*FIVE—(FOUR—THREE—TWO—ONE)*—Jog 2 minutes and stretch out. 1) Jog 5 laps jumping rope; walk one lap 2) Jog 4 laps jumping rope; walk one lap; 3) Jog 3 laps dribbling basketball, walk one lap; 4) Jog 2 laps dribbling basketball, walk one lap; 5) Jog 1 lap dribbling (Repeat for 20 minutes) Cool down.
6.	
Warm Up Workout Cool Down	*SIXTEEN TONS*—Jog 2 laps and stretch out. Participate for 15 minutes in strength circuit (sit-ups; push-ups; bicep curls; tricep presses; 90° squats, etc.) After the circuit, jump rope for 10 minutes. Cool Down.

Topic: Motivation and Achievement

Achievement-related motives affect the ability to do better in activity (V4, P19)

The ability to achieve is regarded as a paramount attribute in today's society. Physical activities often appear to offer the typical aspects of an achievement situation: the outcome is challenging and uncertain; resultant behavior is evaluated by standards; and the participant(s) perceives the outcome as a result of skill and not chance.

Motivation is the key to achievement. Understanding the importance of motivation and knowing how to motivate oneself and others is crucial information for students striving to achieve in motor skill development.

As a result of this learning experience the student should experience improved team effort as a result of motivation instilled by the teacher and incorporated by the group. It should be noted, however, that the elements of experiential learning and practice may also be influential factors leading to successful performance in this lesson, that is, achievement.

Learning Experiences:

Motivation: A stepping stone to achievement

This activity may not be sufficient in content to utilize a complete period. However, it could be used as a warm-up for other activities in the class period.

1. Discuss the concepts from the discussion section and indicate the learning objectives of the lesson. *Do not* tell the students that it is motivation that will improve their performance (assuming it will in this learning experience). Instead, let them discover this for themselves.
2. Indicate that the activity "The Clock" is an anaerobic activity. Discuss or review what anaerobic means. Primarily the activity offers the opportunity of working together (teamwork) to *achieve* in a group setting.
3. Divide the class into groups of tens. Have the members in each individual group join hands. Place four pylons (cones) at the 3, 6, 9 and 12 o'clock positions inside each group circle. The pylons serve as reference points for the starting, reversing, and stopping action involved in the activity.
4. While holding hands, each individual group begins to move in a counterclockwise direction as fast as possible in an effort to get back to the position at which each person started. As soon as that initial starting position is reached everyone in the circle immediately reverses direction (clockwise) and moves as quickly as possible to regain the original position a second time, whereupon the circling stops.

5. When the teacher says "go", and the students in each group start the movements described above, the teacher calls out elapsed seconds in a loud voice. The students listen for the second called out as they finish the task.
6. The teacher then challenges all groups to seek greater achievement, that is, to lower their previous times. This challenge can be made several times. Experience with this activity indicates that results are almost always improved. Intergroup competition can also be instituted if more intensive motivation is desired and appropriate. This sometimes will enhance lowering of times even further.
7. Discuss with the class the phenomenon of lowered (better) times. Ask students to speculate about why the phenomenon occurred. (Claims that practice may have contributed to better times are of course valid, but focus on why they felt they wanted to achieve more in second and third efforts than they did in the initial effort.)
8. Review with the students the components of an achievement situation: the outcome is challenging and uncertain; resultant behavior is evaluated by standards; the participant(s) perceives the outcome as a result of skill not chance.

Materials Needed:

- stopwatch
- pylons (cones)

Evaluation:

1. Ask the class how individuals can self-motivate for better achievement in physical activities in which they are interested.
2. A subjective evaluation of the objectives can be made after discussion.

References:

Rohnke, K. "The Clock." *Cowstails and Cobras.* Hamilton, MA: Project Adventure, p. 21.

Related Concepts:

- Competitiveness is one form of achievement-related behavior (V4, P22)

Topic: Ideas To Enhance Self-Management Of Physical Activity

Perceptions of freedom help individuals feel good (V4, P10)

Time in physical education class is precious and should not be wasted. Research has provided us with information about improving our skill and fitness abilities. In order to improve our aerobic capacity we need to exercise aerobically at least three times per week for 15–45 minutes at our target heart rate. Skill development requires time and appropriate practice. Therefore, the use of class time is very important.

In order for class time to be used most efficiently, students must take responsibility for their own involvement. The learning environment can be set up so that a great deal of choice is available. The privilege of choice assumes adequate skill, fitness, and the ability to be a responsible participant.

The pursuit of an active lifestyle can be facilitated by the teacher, but the ultimate responsibility lies with each student. Self-management is the key.

As a result of this experience, students will understand their responsibility for their own pre-class warm-up. The student will also be able to make choices within a physical education environment and participate fully.

Learning Experiences:

Creating Environments That Promote Choice

1. Explain the idea of self-management and responsible decision-making. Emphasize the importance of making appropriate choices.

2. Explain lesson procedure. For example, the gymnasium may be set up in learning centers. The lesson objectives may include at least 15 minutes of continuous aerobic activity and 10–15 minutes of practice on a sport skill. Students must make choices in order to fulfill satisfactorily each objective.

3. Initially, the teacher may wish to limit the amount of time (last 10 minutes of class) and the number of choices made by the students. However, as students become better decision-makers, create more choices for them and allow more time for the chosen activities. The goal is for students to set specific objectives and to work on them independently.

Materials Needed:

- equipment for each learning center
- pace clock
- self-testing equipment (e.g. sit and reach box, mats for sit-ups)
- "Eight and Five Choice Learning Environments"

Evaluation:

Observation by the teacher is important to monitor behavior. However, students should be responsible for evaluating their own achievement of class (or personal) objectives.

Related Concepts:

- Regular exercise should be tailored to personal needs (V1, P81)
- Personal meaning of movement experience contributes to satisfaction (V5, P42)
- Achieving is more than winning (V5, P16)

EXAMPLE OF AN EIGHT CHOICE LEARNING ENVIRONMENT

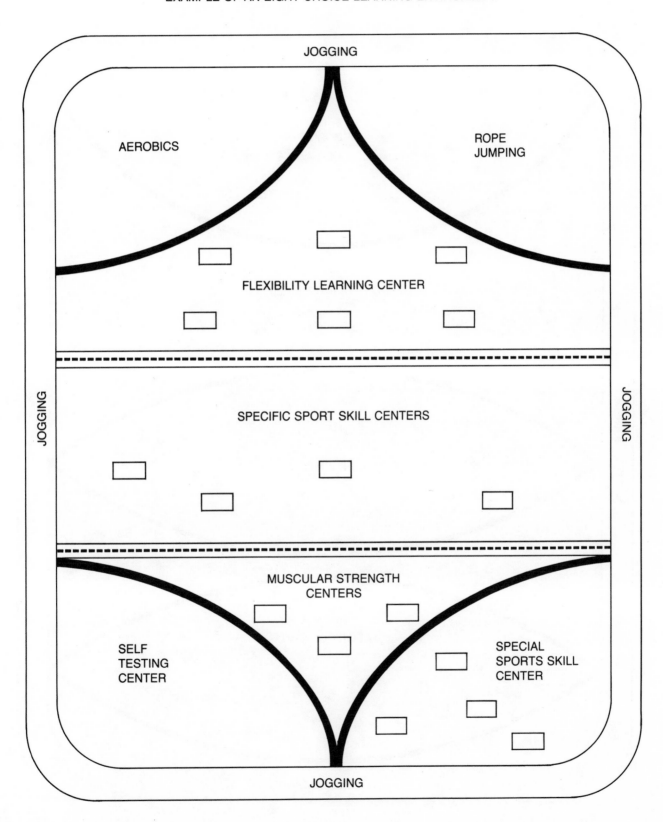

EXAMPLE OF A FIVE CHOICE LEARNING ENVIRONMENT

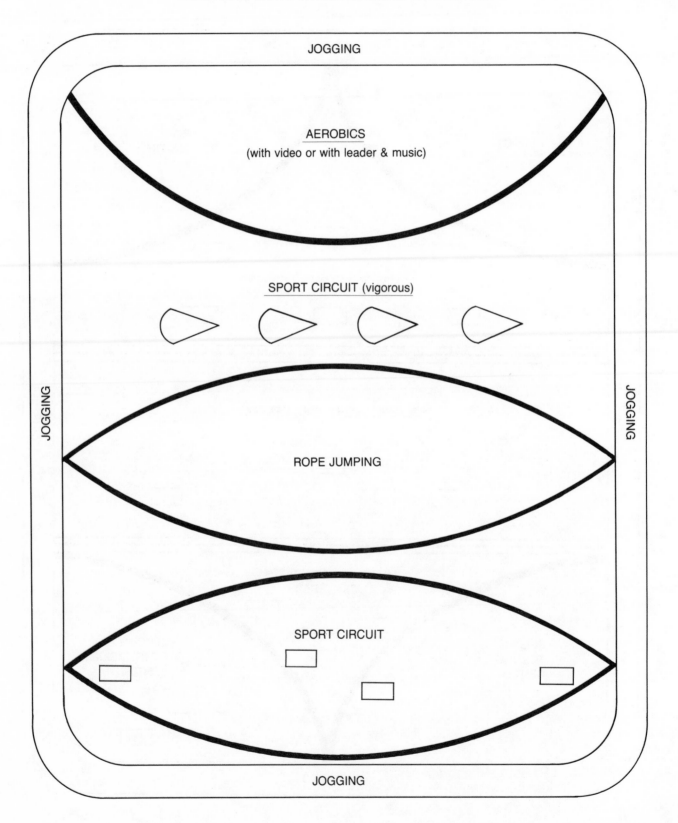

Topic: Experiencing Success: Involving Important Others

Cooperation toward a common goal helps affiliation (V4, P40)

Making physical activity a part of one's life often requires the support of friends and family members. These individuals can serve as positive reinforcers. Without external support, we often stop participating in physical activity. As human beings, we have a basic need to affiliate with others. Significant others serve as a motivating force. When they choose to cooperate with us in achieving a goal, it makes the process of goal attainment more meaningful and more enjoyable.

As a result of this learning experience, the student will be able to involve parents and friends in their physical activity decisions, and will feel as though others share in their achievements and are there to help them through frustrations.

Learning Experiences:

Involving Parents

1. This is a take home activity which is monitored by parents. Explain the idea of affiliation and the importance of others.
2. This activity actually educates the parents about your program and may spark their interest in their child's development. Furthermore, it may plant a seed which, when nurtured, incorporates physical activity into the family's lifestyle. (*Ned Pinkerton in Jackson, Wyoming effectively uses this idea in his program.*)

Materials Needed:

- "Here's Our Team Plan"
- "Activity Calendar"
- "Tips for Exercise"

Evaluation:

Feedback from parents should provide a very rich program evaluation information. Students should be asked to return the log portion of the packet each month.

Related Concepts:

- Proximity has a positive affect on affiliation (V4, P40)
- Participation in physical activity can be an important way of meeting affiliation needs (V4, P38)
- Affiliation is a very important human need (V4, P37)
- Satisfaction results from attaining goals (V6, P57)

CAN BE PART OF OUR TEAM!

HERE'S OUR TEAM PLAN . . .

Research in Physical Education has consistently shown that in order to be effective, physical activity must be performed three or more times a week. Our physical education schedule is limited to two class meetings per week. Our combined efforts of home activity and class activity will provide your children with a well balanced fitness program.

✔ I will provide a well balanced variety of fitness related activities in class.

✔ The students will participate in class and choose a suitable fitness activity to do at home.

✔ You are invited to encourage your child's activity and to initial a progress chart to be returned to school.

★★FITNESS HAS NO SEASON. IT IS AN ON-GOING PROCESS THROUGHOUT THE YEAR, THROUGHOUT LIFE!

Activity Calendar

STUDENTS: Color in a space for every day you
have done a fitness activity

PARENTS: Fill in the calendar and initial the days
your child has done a fitness activity

*NOTE: Do not count Physical Education class
as a fitness activity on these charts

	Sunday	Monday	Tuesday	Wednesday	Thursday	Friday	Saturday
TIME OR AMOUNT							
ACTIVITY							
TIME OR AMOUNT							
ACTIVITY							
TIME OR AMOUNT							
ACTIVITY							
TIME OR AMOUNT							
ACTIVITY							
TIME OR AMOUNT							
ACTIVITY							

NAME: _____

MONTH: _____

TIPS FOR EXERCISING

Warm-up: Two to three minutes of activity to warm the entire body. (Jumping jacks, rope jumping, jogging in place, and so on)

Light Stretch: Three to four minutes of easy stretching for 30 seconds or more. Slow rotation of joints. (Ankles, shoulder area, arms, wrist, and so on) *A more thorough total body stretch comes at the end of an activity.*

Heart Endurance Activity:

  What To Do?   Aerobic dance (video or live), quick walk, jump rope, bike riding (stationary or on the road), jog, roller skate, cross-country skiing.

  How Hard?   So you can still talk to someone while exercising.

  How Long?   30 minutes without stopping is the goal. However, if you are just starting, 5 minutes is good. Increase your time 5 minutes each week until you are at 30 minutes.

  How Often?   Two or three days a week. If possible select days you do not have physical education.

Have Fun With It!   Pick an activity you like! Change activities whenever you want, but *be active.* Try to plan your activity for the same time each day so it becomes part of your life.

Cool Down: Slow down to an easy (walk) pace and continue for around three to five minutes.

Total Body Stretch: Now is the time to stretch out all the muscles you used. Slow deep stretch for several minutes concentrating on the specific muscles used.

Topic: Competitive Stress and Skill Performance

Competitive stress affects performance in physical activity (V4, P26)

Note: This activity should precede discussion of the topic and the objectives of this learning experience.

The level of anxiety common to all individuals is called *trait anxiety*. The level of anxiety experienced in any specific situation is called *state anxiety*. *Competitive trait anxiety* is the tendency to perceive any competitive situation as threatening.

All performers have *optimal arousal levels*. An optimal arousal level is one that maintains the interest level of the performer without making the activity stressful. High competitive stress can cause performance breakdown in some people, while others require it in order to maintain arousal level. It is important that the individual characteristics and reactions to competitive stress be understood by students and teachers.

As a result of this learning experience the student should recognize the effects of stress on the performance of individuals.

Learning Experiences:

The effect of competition on performance

1. In this learning experience some subterfuge is required as well as a deviation from the normal effort to maximize participation. Therefore, it is suggested that when using this lesson that the activity be engaged in first, with the discussion occurring in the closing phase of the lesson.
2. The lesson should be initiated with the pretense that the game is being played for the purpose of getting the students to learn more about each other. Students' names, favorite cars, favorite foods, or favorite sports could be used as a theme for the activity.
3. This activity could be called "Chalkboard Relay," "Information Relay," or "Get Acquainted Relay." The teacher divides the class into 4–8 teams. Each team is asked to decide who will be the first participant on the team (lead-off), who will be second, third, and fourth (anchor). In the order decided, the students will then either print or write their responses to the theme of the relay (see above: this could be name, favorite car, etc., but the same theme is used by all participants). The students then go to a pre-arranged starting point directly opposite their space on the chalkboard.

4. The relay activity itself can involve any skill desired. For example, the first people in each line on the word "go", dribble the ball to the chalkboard, place the ball on the floor, write or print whatever they wrote in the space above. Other variations might include "skating" to the board on carpet squares, dribbling a soccer ball etc. The traditional relay format is used.

5. Encourage team members to call out the names, cars, or whatever the theme idea is as teammates move to and from the board. Ostensibly this is done to better remember the specific information. Actually this is done to interject more stimuli into the task.

6. When the relay is over, have the students move forward to positions so that the content on the chalkboard can be seen easily. The teacher then conveys to the learners the salient points made in the discussion section and indicates the objective of the lesson.

7. The teacher explains the subterfuge used, and, using what appears on the board discusses the following.
   a. Teacher identifies significant differences in the quality of printing (or writing) between the non-competitive phase and the competitive phase. Why did such differences occur? What significance might this have for using competitive activities in the teaching/learning process?
   b. What reasons can be given as to why the quality of the printing (or writing) did not vary between the competitive and non-competitive phases for some people?
   c. Was there any visible concern or discussion within each group as to who would go first, last, etc.? Discuss the possibilities of this with regard to stress.
   d. Ask for individual opinions regarding situations in which they experienced stress in physical education or sports activities, both inside or outside of class.
   e. Ask what effect they feel stress has on learning.
   f. Ask students to share their personal feelings about competition.

Materials Needed:

- portable chalkboard, chalk, and eraser
- one ball or set of carpet squares for each team

Evaluation:

1. The teacher subjectively will evaluate student input and insight with regard to items a and b above.
2. The teacher subjectively will evaluate other conceptual understanding that is noted.

Related Concepts:

- Competitiveness is one form of achievement-related behavior (V4, P22)
- Stress reduction can help in doing better (V4, P33)
- Fear of failure affects performance in physical activity (V4, P20)

Chalkboard Relay			
Team 1	Team 2	Team 3	Team 4
1. Bill	Jack	Tom	Del
2. Claudia	Phyllis	Margaret	Tracey
3. Beth	Brant	Sean	Tim
4. Julie	Jill	Laurie	Thomas
1.			
2.			
3.			
4.			
Team #1	Team #2	Team #3	Team #4
X	X	X	X
X	X	X	X
X	X	X	X
X	X	X	X

AN INVITATION
FROM AAHPERD/NASPE

The American Alliance for Health, Physical Education, Recreation, and Dance, NASPE, and the many *Basic Stuff* authors cordially invite *you* to become a participating author and to design or share current learning experiences with other professionals throughout the United States. Using the format guidelines on the following page, please complete your Learning Experience, indicate your name and professional affiliation, and mail it to:

Acquisitions Editor
Basic Stuff Project
AAHPERD
1900 Association Drive
Reston, VA 22091

As soon as we have an adequate number of Learning Experiences, we will publish them under a title such as *The Best of Basic Stuff*.

Topic:_____

Grade Level: ☐ K–3   ☐ 4–8   ☐ 9–12

Goal: ☐ Personal Fitness   ☐ Skillful Moving   ☐ Joy, Pleasure, & Satisfaction

Concept:_____

_____ volume _____ page _____

Discussion (*introduction to concept, definitions, relationships, purposes, outcomes, etc.*):_____

_____

_____

_____

Conceptual Focus (*What are the main points of this topic?*):

1. _____

_____

2. _____

_____

3. _____

_____

Learning Experiences (*includes tasks, classwork, labs, homework, etc.—small tables, charts, and worksheets included here*):

1. _____

_____

2. _____

_____

3. _____

_____

Materials Needed:

● _____

● _____

● _____

Evaluation:

1. _____

_____

2. _____

_____

References (*need only if very specific references used or suggested*):

_____

_____

Related Concepts:

● _____ volume _____ page _____

● _____ volume _____ page _____

● _____ volume _____ page _____

Attach additional full page lab experiences, worksheets, take-homes, transparencies, duplicating masters, and other materials

Annotated Bibliography
(Grades 4–8)

Bird, A. M., Cripe, B. K., & Morrison, N. L. (1980). Children and stress. *JOPER, 51*(5), 28–29, 62.
This article gives suggestions and ideas for implementing stress coping techniques and teaching methods to help minimize stressful feelings occurring in physical education classes.

Bunk, C. (1980). Muscle of the week. *JOPER, 51*(7), 79.
A description of a program called, "muscle of the week" that was implemented at an elementary school. Each week a specific muscle's name, spelling, easy ways to remember it, ideas of how to stretch and strengthen the muscle were explored and practiced, and relevant sports and activities which used that muscle were studied.

Calvin, C. (1974). Movement education and soccer. *Physical Educator, 31*(3), 148–150.
Teaching concepts underlying movement education (i.e., time, space, force) in application to developing sports skills. Examples of relating the importance of these concepts to the game of soccer are given.

Campbell, W. C. (1977). A high school physical fitness testing kit. *JOPER, 48*(1), 38.
A brief description of a kit developed to allow students to test their own physical fitness. The kit includes charts, equipment, evaluation forms, result forms, loop films, and a teacher's manual.

Capon, J. (1974). Group activities to reinforce body image development. *JOHPER, 45*(9), 82–83.
Ideas and suggested activities for teaching children concepts of body image, which involves knowledge of the physical structure, the movements, functions, and position of the body, and its parts in relation to each other.

Carlisle, C. (1986). Dance curriculum for elementary children: Using a scientific approach. *JOPERD, 57*(5), 31, 54.
Description of an approach to teaching educational dance to elementary students through the combined use of biomechanical principles, movement themes, and fundamental movement skills.

Carlson, J. B. (1979). Extending the boundaries of the imagination. *JOPER, 50*(4), 28–29.
Story of a teacher's assignment to 7th graders of a project involving defining and giving examples of words such as human movement, dance, force, space, agility, time.

Corbin, C. B. (1978). Changing consumers mean new concepts. *JOPER, 49*(1), 43.
Several brief examples of how concepts programs have been implemented in secondary schools and the benefits to students, parents, and school officials.

Corbin, C. B. (Ed.). (1970). The "why" of physical activity. *Physical Educator, 27*(4), 37–38.
The "why" of physical activity is something everyone should know and is not something that can be assumed is understood. Physical educators must make a conscious effort to teach these values and concepts.

Crawford, S. (1984). The celluloid athlete. Sports movies as teaching tools. *JOPERD, 55*(8), 24–27.
The author suggests using films for analyzing major issues in sport and society. Selected movies are placed in six categories and basic thematic issues for discussion and analysis are identified.

DeSorbe, B. M. (1977). How do you get the ball from here to there? *JOPER, 48*(6), 35–36.
Description of ways to teach elementary children about angles and trajectories of balls.

Edington, D. W., & Cunningham, L. (1973). Applied physiology of exercise: A biological awareness concept. *JOHPER, 44*(8), 30–31.
Specific suggestions of ways to teach exercise physiology concepts in elementary physical education. Examples of topics such as energy metabolism, respiration, and cardiovascular dynamics are given.

Hartman, B., & Clement, A. (1973). Adventure in key concepts. *JOHPER, 44*(3), 20–22.
An explanation of the process used for developing the Ohio Guide for Girls Secondary Physical Education. The key concepts of movement performance, cognitive understanding, and affective sensation became the unifying force for guiding and selecting learning activities.

Heitman, H. (1984). Physical education for survival: Back to basics. *JOPERD, 55*(6), 25–26.
The article questions the current focus in physical education on sport education and proposes a curriculum which encompasses both the structure of the discipline and the utilitarian and recreational integration of skills and knowledge. Specific suggestions are given about teaching principles of balance and leverage as a part of a life safety/risk unit.

Herkowitz, J. (1970). A perceptual motor training program to improve the gross motor abilities of preschoolers. *JOHPER, 41*(4), 38–42.
A discussion of some activities developed for use in a perceptual-motor training laboratory in hopes of enhancing preschoolers perceptual-motor behavior and concepts.

Hinds, J. (1971). Body orientation: A workable technique for self-discovery. *JOHPER, 42*(1), 44, 57.
Ideas for teaching biomechanical principles such as force absorption, force production, and body rotation to students.

Horrocks, R. (1980). Sportsmanship and moral reasoning. *Physical Educator, 37*(4), 208–212.
The author discusses several ways to enhance the development of a child's social learning and cognitive development. He suggests setting up reciprocal teaching situations, having open discussions on sportsmanship and value clarifications, or creating a laboratory in which students can interact and share ideas in developing original games.

Horrocks, R. N. (1977). Sportsmanship. *JOPER, 48*(9), 20–21.
The author uses a direct approach to teaching sportsmanship through the use of a

series of hypothetical moral dilemmas in stories about games, sports, and contests. The stories are used to stimulate questions and discussions among 5th and 6th grade students.

Jenkins, D. (1977). Muscle of the month. *JOPER, 48*(3), 30.
A brief description of an elementary teacher introducing the study of muscles and their function in his physical education classes.

Jenkins, D. (1985). Student fitness. The physical educator's role. *JOPERD, 56*(2), 31–32.
Two teachers outline their goals for the development of physical fitness in their students. One major goal is "fitness education," that is, students must understand the "why" as well as "how to" of exercise.

Krampf, H., Hopkins, D., & Byrd, J. (1979). Muscular relaxation for the elementary student. *JOPER, 50*(4), 70–71.
A brief explanation of a strategy for teaching relaxation to elementary students. The program consists of a series of guided lessons to assist students in becoming aware of their tension and how to release the tensions.

McColl, S. L. (1979). Dance as aesthetic education. *JOPER, 50*(7), 44–46.
Article describes how dance can develop its potential as an aesthetic experience through utilizing and combining 5 areas: basic aesthetic elements, images, composing, the flow of movement sequences, and wholeness created by structuring the learning process.

Melograno, V. (1984). The balanced curriculum—Where is it? What is it? *JOPERD, 55*(6), 21–24, 52.
When developing curriculum, teaching concepts from physical education's body of knowledge is one way suggested of providing a balanced curriculum.

Melville, S. (1985). Teaching and evaluating cognitive skills in elementary physical education. *JOPERD, 56*(2), 26–28.
A teacher describes how to integrate the teaching and testing of Basic Stuff concepts in a physical education class for 3rd and 4th graders.

Mohr, D. R. (1971). Identifying the body of knowledge. *JOHPER, 42*(1), 23–24.
A discussion of the need for expanding physical education classes to include the "why" of performance. Three specific examples are given for implementing conceptual learning in physical education classes.

Ratliffe, T. (1982). Using worksheets in physical education. *JOPERD, 53*(7), 47–48.
A description of a teacher who believes that cognitive understanding enhances the learning of physical skills and uses worksheets to enhance this learning.

Schueler, A. (1979). The inquiry model in physical education. *Physical Educator, 36*(2), 89–91.
A description of an experimental unit using inquiry into problems in sport. Students first determined topics (e.g., athletes should be allowed to take drugs, girls develop masculine traits in some sports, violence should be a part of sports), then researched the topics (in groups), and reported to the class. An alternative to both command style teaching and a curriculum based on sports skills.

Shadduck, I. G. (1970). Johnston research project—a curriculum based on concepts. *Physical Educator, 27*(3), 107–109.
Description of an experimental project on curriculum in physical education titled, "The Development, Implementation, and Evaluation of Teaching-Learning Materials Based on a Conceptual Approach to Physical Education."

Spindt, G. (1985). Fitness is basic. *JOPERD, 56*(7), 68–69.
Description of a fitness program at a junior high which emphasizes both increasing students' fitness levels and students' understanding of concepts of fitness and its relationship to a healthy lifestyle.

St. Clair, S. I. (1986). Innovation—the answer to overcrowded classes. *JOPERD, 57*(8), 62.
Teaching several mini-units in sport history (basketball, baseball) as part of a rotating schedule is one teacher's solution to lack of space and too many students.

Wasserman, B. (1970). Universal moves in gymnastics. *Physical Educator, 27*(3), 118–119.
Ideas for teaching gymnasts concepts of movement so they will better understand what is involved in different gymnastic stunts.

Werner, P. H. (1982). Concept teaching in movement and music. *JOPERD, 53*(7), 48–49.
A description of a program in which a physical education teacher and a music teacher combine forces to teach elementary students concepts such as space, force, and rhythm through units such as "How the Body Moves—Characteristics of Sound and Rhythm."

Wyckoff, W. L. (1980). Movement programs and aesthetic education. *JOPER, 51*(4), 65–67.
Overview of background of current national interest in the aesthetic content of school curriculum. Body of article states the broad general goals of aesthetic education curriculums and describes some relevant aesthetic content inherent in movement programs.

Evaluation Form

After some experience with using this book, please complete and return this evaluation form so that you can help us improve our books. Send completed form to:

> AAHPERD Acquisitions Editor
> Basic Stuff Project
> 1900 Association Drive
> Reston, VA 22091

- -

1. This book is from: _____ Series I or _____ Series II

2. The name of the book is:
   _____

3. I found the information to be: (Please include specific comments on the reverse side of this form.)

   Accurate   _____ : _____ : _____ : _____ : _____   Inaccurate

   Confusing   _____ : _____ : _____ : _____ : _____   Understandable

   Helpful   _____ : _____ : _____ : _____ : _____   Not Helpful

   Useable   _____ : _____ : _____ : _____ : _____   Not Useable

4. Please identify some of the reasons which lead you to purchase this book:

   a. _____

   b. _____

   c. _____

5. What do you wish the authors would have included in this book?

   a. _____

   b. _____

   c. _____

THANK YOU for your comments! We rely on your opinions to help us improve the *Basic Stuff* Series in the years to come.